DISCIPLING THE AFRICAN AMERICAN MALE

*How to get black men into church
and keep them there*

DR. LARRY L. MACON

Goo Bless You!

James C. Winston

Publishing Company, Inc.

Trade Division of Winston-Derek Publishers Group, Inc.

TO SOW THE FALLOW SOIL

First printing

The material contained in Appendix Two is from *Black History Activity and Enrichment Handbook*, edited by Wade Hudson and Cheryl Willis Hudson (New Jersey: Just Us Books, 1990), 40-41. Used by permission of the publisher.

The material contained in Appendices Three, Four, Five, Eight, and Nine is from *The Black Male: The New Bald Eagle*, by Jeffrey M. Johnson (Washington: Management Plus, 1989), 81. Used by permission of the publisher.

The material contained in Appendices Six and Seven is from *Black Men: Obsolete, Single, Dangerous?*, by Haki R. Madhubuti (Chicago: Third World Press, 1990). Used by permission of the publisher.

The material contained in Appendix Ten is based upon *Dimensions of Spirituality in the Black Experience, Leader's Guide*, by Robert E. Dungy, copyright 1991. Used by permission of the publisher, The Upper Room, 1908 Grand Avenue, P. O. Box 189, Nashville, TN 37202.

The material contained in Appendices Twelve, Thirteen, Fourteen, and Fifteen is from *Partners in Ministry: Laity & Pastors Working Together*, by James L. Garlow (Kansas City: Beacon Hill Press, 1981), Appendix B, resource sheets numbers 2, 2B, and 7B. Used by permission of the publisher.

PUBLISHED BY JAMES C. WINSTON PUBLISHING COMPANY, INC.
Nashville, Tennessee 37205

Library of Congress Catalog Card No: 94-61589
ISBN: 1-55523-733-9

Printed in the United States of America

To my mother and father, Delina and Louis Macon,
who taught me how to become a man of God.

Contents

Acknowledgments

There are those to whom I owe debts too lengthy to acknowledge here. However, I wish to especially thank the following people who gave me ideas, directions, resources, and encouragement throughout my Doctor of Ministry program: Dr. Richard E. Allison, Director of Doctoral Studies; Dr. Marvin A. McMickle, field consultant; Dr. Arthur E. Kemp, resource person; Dr. Fred Holland, peer group leader; and Dr. Otis Moss, Jr. and Dr. Andrew Edwards, faculty members at the McCreary Center for Black Church Studies. I would like to express my sincere thanks to Dr. William H. Myers, my academic adviser, who met with me many times for consultations and gave me helpful insights that made for better reading and understanding of my project.

Also, I wish to express my deepest appreciation to my wife, Marilyn, and my two sons, Larry Jr. and Daniel, for their patience and love. My debt to them will never be met in this life.

To Dr. Henry Payden, Sr., Dr. Douglas M. Little, C. J. Matthews, and Emery Ivery, I extend special thanks for their friendship and constant words of encouragement.

Finally, I want to thank the members and friends of the Mt. Zion Baptist Church of Oakwood Village, Ohio, for their patience, prayers, and the many privileges they extended to me during this time.

Introduction

The Gospel of Matthew records an incident in which the Sadducees approached Jesus and posed a difficult question regarding marriage. "Suppose," they asked, "a woman had married seven brothers in succession. Whose wife would she be at the resurrection?" Jesus informed them that in heaven, people "neither marry, nor are given in marriage."[1] Historically, a black preacher might have substantiated Jesus' claim by humorously adding that there are no marriages in heaven because there are so few men in heaven. These same preachers would then argue that there are few men in heaven because there are few men in church. Unfortunately, this observation would not be far from the truth. According to some studies, males are less interested in religious activities than females.[2] And even when men are present at the church, they are often uninvolved in the ministry. In *Until the Men Sit Down*, Clifford E. McLain states that black men are "found on the periphery, detached and practically religiously illiterate."[3] I disagree with the conclusion that there will be few men in heaven because few men attend church. However, an active church membership *is* a good sign of one's rightful relationship and fellowship with God. The Apostle

John speaks of having fellowship one with another as a clear sign of fellowship with God.[4] In addition, the writer of Hebrews says:

> And let us consider one another to provoke unto love and to good works: not forsaking the assembling of ourselves together, as the manner of some is; but exhorting one another: and so much the more, as you see the day approaching.[5]

The Great Commission given by Christ in Matthew 28:19-20 is to lead all people to the saving power of Jesus Christ. Once those people are saved, they are to be discipled (Matt. 4:17-22; Mark 1:14-20). Thus, if men are not actively attending church, it is the church's responsibility to identify those men, lead them to Christ, and make them his disciples.

It is with this goal in mind that this book will develop a model for discipling the African American male. His lack of presence and participation, except in small numbers, in the ministry of the church is noticeable and disturbing. In comparison to women and children, few men can be found worshipping on any given Sunday. I confirmed this absence of men in the church through personal interviews with leading black pastors and scholars (Dr. Otis Moss of Olivet Institutional Baptist Church in Cleveland, Ohio; Dr. Marvin McMickle, pastor of Antioch Baptist Church in Cleveland, Ohio; Dr. William A. Jones of Bethany Baptist Church in Brooklyn, New York; Dr. Samuel Proctor of Abyssinian Baptist Church in New York City; Dr. C. Eric Lincoln, noted "Dean of Black Religion" and author; Dr. Kelly Brown of Howard University; and Dr. Gayraud Wilmore, noted author and scholar). All over America, pastors, theologians, and scholars are asking a similar question: "Where are the men, and how can they be discipled?"

If we could develop a strategy to attract black men and ensure their participation in the church's ministry, more black families might be drawn to the church. McLain points out that the black church at the local level seems too slow in expressing concern regarding this decline in black male membership.[6] Furthermore, as the black male presence in the church decreases in visibility and function, the black church may also decline in visibility. In fact, McLain predicts that by the year 2000, black women in the church may outnumber black men thirty- or forty-to-one if this trend continues.[7] All of the pastors, theologians, and scholars interviewed admitted that, at present, females far outnumber the males in their churches.

As a child growing up in a traditional black Baptist church, I always questioned why so few African American men attended church. I noticed that the women played an active role in church, but virtually the only men I ever saw on Sundays were preachers, deacons, and a few male choir members. As a result, like many African Americans today, I began thinking that the church was for women and children.[8]

While pastoring the Mt. Zion Baptist Church of Oakwood Village, Ohio for the past fifteen years, I noticed that there were many female and children worshippers and very few male worshippers. At times I attributed this problem to the televised sports events, such as football and baseball games, that usually aired on Sundays. And on those Sundays on which there were no sports events, I assumed that the men were tired and overworked and thus could not attend church services. However, when I considered the heavy workload of women both in and out of the home, I knew this could not be the answer. I knew that the men's lack of participation in the church ministry was not due to a lack of black men in the general population or in my particular city. All I had to do was drive along any inner-city street to see numerous black men lined up along the street curbs.

In time, I began to reflect upon the historical roots and dynamics of the traditional African family. The family was headed by the male, who dominated and led the family in religious practices. During slavery in America, the black male was even considered the religious priest of his household. Therefore, the issue of the lack of a black male presence in today's church became a key concern to me. Black males, like everyone else, need to be saved and discipled. Jesus' message in the gospels includes discipling "all" and involves a commitment to worship, service, and ministry. Such a commitment, I reasoned, would enable black people to rebuild strong churches and families.

The goal of this book, in particular, is to offer a model for discipling black males. It explores the significant variables that impact the involvement of black men in church and uses those variables to construct the model. In designing such a model, one must ask the following questions: why aren't more men attending church? Why aren't more men active in the church's ministry? How can the church attract more men and encourage them to become active disciples? After determining the answers to these questions, such a model could answer another set of questions that has been asked of the church:

1. Where are the men, and why aren't they in church?
2. Why has the church generally accepted the male absence in church and not challenged it or created programs to reach black men?
3. Why is there an apparently natural female and child orientation to religion and to church attendance?
4. Why is there, at times, tension between male and female relationships in the consideration of church attendance and participation?

This work has four objectives: (1) to establish the biblical and theological basis for discipling black males; (2) to increase one's sensitivity to the plight of the black male and the black family; (3) to analyze other models in the country; and (4) to create a working model and manual for the church.

Part One:

Discipleship

Chapter One:

Biblical and Theological Mandates

Jesus said, "Why do you call me, 'Lord, Lord,' and yet don't do what I tell you? Anyone who comes to me, and listens to my words, and obeys them is a true disciple. The true disciple is like one who, in building his house, dug deep and laid the foundation on rock. The river flooded over and hit that house but could not shake it because it was well built. But anyone who hears my words and does not obey them is like a man who built his house without laying a foundation; when the flood hit that house it fell at once—and what a terrible crash that was."[1]

Discipleship has historical and theological roots that can be traced back to the Old Testament. One cannot rightly look at discipleship in the New Testament without seeing it through the lenses of Old Testament theology. There are examples of discipleship in the books of Exodus and Genesis, which offer accounts of six men and their personal relationships with God: Adam, Noah, Abraham, Isaac, Jacob, and Joseph. Exodus teaches us God's model of deliverance from bondage through a mediator. In the Old Testament, this mediator is Moses, and in the New Testament, it is Jesus Christ. Thus, the first key element in becoming a disciple of God is deliverance from the power of darkness into the kingdom of God. The second key element pertains to God's blessing and provision for the redeemed.[2]

The word "disciple" ("mathetes") means a pupil, a learner, or one who follows a religious teacher and is involved in an intimate relationship with that teacher.

> The noun "mathetes," disciple, comes from the verb man-thanein, to learn. It implies personal participation in that which teacher or experience may teach one. These Greek words call to mind the schools of Greek philosophy. Young boys would go to live with a Greek philosopher and learn from his teachings.[3]

Moreover, "disciple" is more often used in the gospels and does not occur in the epistles, perhaps because the word saint ("hagios") replaced the word disciple.[4] Christian discipleship is strict adherence to Christ and following in his footsteps. It involves a process whereby teacher and pupil are molded together as one. This occurs when the true disciples *come, listen,* and *obey.*

COME

We cannot properly undertake a study of discipleship without first considering the call of the disciple. The first request of the disciple is to come.[5] Jesus said that a true disciple is one "who comes to me....Come with me, and I will make you fishers of men."[6] "Follow me, and let the dead bury their dead."[7] "Get up, and pick up your bed, and go home!"[8] "Go and preach, 'The Kingdom of heaven is near!'"[9] "Come to me, all of you who are tired from carrying heavy loads, and I will give you rest."[10] "If anyone wants to come with me, he must forget himself, carry his cross, and follow me."[11] "Let the children come to me."[12]

The vast number of words spoken by Jesus commanding pilgrimage cannot be mere coincidence. At the core of the Christian faith is a living Lord who says "come," "follow," and "go." We must further understand that these mandates of discipleship were meant not only for those first century disciples who could touch and feel the very essence of God through Jesus Christ but for all who would be his disciples. Certainly, it was easier for those first disciples to respond to Jesus' invitation to "come" because of his physical presence. However, that same call still goes forth to modern disciples. Accompanying this command to "come" are three complementary commands:

1. Christian disciples must come to Jesus Christ.
2. Christian disciples must come one with the other.
3. Christian disciples must come to their authentic self.

Christian disciples must come to Jesus Christ. The Christian pilgrimage necessitates that one must first come to Jesus Christ. This is perhaps the most obvious part of the disciple's journey. Furthermore, the concept of discipleship is a dependent one, meaning that disciples cannot be disciples unto themselves and that to come into the state of discipleship is to come to Christ. In *The Equipping of Disciples,* John Hendrix and Lloyd Householder state that "the Christian's lifelong commitment to the person, teaching, and Spirit of Jesus Christ…involves progressive learning, growth in Christlikeness, implementation of biblical truth, and responsibility for sharing the Christian faith."[13] Such a life demands an interaction both with the Jesus of history as he is revealed in the Gospels and with the Christ of faith as he is experienced in one's personal life.

> The expression "creative discipleship" sounds initially somewhat paradoxical. If persons become disciples, they allow themselves to be determined by the one they follow. They imitate their leader, but they are not themselves creative. This impression is false, however. Discipleship is not imitation. Jesus did not call his disciples to imitate him but to participate in his messianic mission: "Preach as you go, saying, 'The Kingdom of heaven is at hand.' Heal the sick, raise the dead, cleanse lepers, cast out demons" (Matt. 10:7). They are not called upon to help him carry his cross,

but to take up their own cross (Matt. 10:38). The call to discipleship is therefore a call to responsible maturity in fellowship—yes, even friendship—with Jesus.[14]

It is inappropriate to presume that one becomes a disciple apart from Christ. To come to Christ means to join Christ in life and ministry.

One becomes united with Christ by way of a personal redemption experience through the grace of God.[15] The Gospel of Mark illustrates the distinction between being saved versus discipleship.[16] In other words, true discipleship goes beyond being saved—it is being of service and joining oneself to Christ in holiness, attitude, motivation, personal relationship, and conduct. It is living under his authority and living by faith.[17] The prerequisite to becoming a disciple, as T. M. Moore shares, is as follows:

> The individual called to be a disciple of Jesus Christ is summoned to a lifestyle that is all-encompassing and unique. Scripture tells us that those who belong to Jesus have been "born again," have entered into an existence in which "old things have passed away...all things have become new," and are called upon to "be transformed by the renewing of your mind, that you may prove what is that good and acceptable and perfect will of God." We are told that the "all things" of a disciple's life and experience become the possession of his Lord, and that he is called upon to learn how to serve as a steward over these "all things" in the world God has made. This calling to discipleship as a steward over one's life for God requires a self-conscious and persistent effort to "do all to the glory of God."[18]

Thus, the word disciple means learner, or apprentice. By definition, the disciples of Christ follow him, and in so doing, grow into his likeness. For Jesus, the words "follower" and "disciple" were interchangeable. Disciples are followers in the sense that they journey where Christ is already present. Therefore, followers must learn at the "feet of Christ."

Hendrix and Householder offer the following insights:

> First, there is the calling out, the invitation to follow, to join the journey, to begin the pilgrimage, to experience: Jesus called individuals to follow in a special way, to experience his life with him: to watch, to observe, to listen, to reflect. When he healed, they observed. When he debated, they reflected. When he dialogued with individuals, they listened. Then he sent them out to experience firsthand what he was doing, to implement, to experiment. And to learn from both success and failure....First experience, then reflection and observation (what happened and what did it mean), then the principles, then experimentation with the principles, then experimentation with the principle which led to a new experience.[19]

Christian disciples must also come one with the other. It should be no surprise to discover that Christian discipleship does not occur in isolation. Discipleship is not a journey to be attempted alone; there are too many problems, obstacles, deterrences, and risks along the way. The spirit who guides, leads, and protects also avails himself wherever "two or three are gathered in my name."[20] Discipleship, then, is not only dependent on a relationship with Christ, but it also involves fellowship with one another.

This journey of Christ's disciple is not merely one to be traveled alongside each other; rather, one journeys in a fellowship. The Gospel of Mark says the disciples were sent out two by two.[21] This arrangement is also reflected in Matthew's gospel when he lists the twelve in pairs.[22] The early church followed this one-to-one practice as well in pairing Paul and Barnabas, Barnabas and Mark, and Paul and Silas.[23]

This coming together of people is characterized by intimacy and accountability, two qualities that the local church often fails at acquiring. Intimacy requires an honesty that moves beyond the superficial formality that characterizes many churches.

> Jesus confronts those who will listen and challenges them to *change radically* in a *context of support*. This is the milieu

11

of the perceptual shift which is Christian growth. If either [part] of this two-sided message is lost, the creative impetus of the message suffers. Challenge without support becomes threatening judgment; support without challenge, a secure womb.[24]

Furthermore, the local church often fails even more through its lack of accountability. The church has been seen for too long as a volunteer army where discipleship is an option and accountability is often viewed as an intrusion. Coppedge maintains that

there are two kinds of accountability. One is judgmental and tends to be strict and impersonal while focusing primarily upon performance. The other is supportive and challenging. The latter is more like the New Testament model that was designed to encourage and build up those seeking to be disciples. This pattern holds people accountable so that they may grow by discipline.[25]

Coppedge informs his reader that discipleship is defined in terms of accountability, discipline, practice, and life transference. He says that for true discipleship to occur, there must be accountability to other believers—accountability that is simultaneously supportive and challenging. There must be discipline in the continual use of Bible reading, giving, prayer, and worship. Finally, there must be "life transference," whereby a person sees, experiences, evaluates, and finally emulates a perceived model of discipleship.[26] Coppedge supports this position with the paradigm of Jesus in discipling the Twelve:

The biblical picture of God's objectives for Jesus' disciples is Christlikeness of character, fruitfulness in service, and an intimate relationship with the Lord. His chief means to accomplish these ends are the experience of saving grace, sanctifying grace, and growth in grace.[27]

In other words, for Coppedge, the means to accomplishing God's end of true discipleship is a born-again experience, an "in-filling" of the Holy Spirit, which leads to proper accountability and intimacy.

Hence, as Coppedge further adds:

> Accountability is crucial for any kind of serious training
> and discipling. Disciples are to account for themselves. The
> twelve are accountable to Jesus for almost every aspect of
> their lives in as much as they move in his immediate pres-
> ence all the time....He checks up on them when they
> return from missions on which he sends them (Mark
> 6:7-13, 30; Luke 9:1-6, 10). As part of life-to-life transfer-
> ence, they live and work together while Jesus sends them
> two by two. Part of the reason for ministry teams is fellow-
> ship and encouragement, but another part is accountabil-
> ity. No disciple is completely on his own, but is responsible
> to a larger group committed to the same purposes.[28]

Another reason for the need for intimacy and accountability in the
local church has to do with humanity's fallen nature and the need for
support. Sin has affected human motives and desires, and as a result,
Christians need to be accountable to other believers in order to help
them do what they really desire to do and that which they know God
desires them to do. Being accountable means that members of the
body of Christ care enough for one another to hold each other responsible for practices that result in a rightful relationship with God.[29]
Such accountability creates both a vertical (God to man) and a hori-
zontal (man to man) relationship that facilitates true discipleship.
Hence, disciples can hold each other accountable to their journey and
can do so without imposing one's way, or even what one assumes to
be God's way.

Hendrix and Householder add a moral dimension to the meaning
of discipleship when coming together. They are of the opinion that
within the process of discipleship, there is the goal of achieving moral
maturation. To them, Jesus' moral maturation could be described as
moving from imperfection to perfection, or from brokenness to wholeness. The authors support this stance from a biblical basis, namely the
Beatitudes of Jesus found in Matthew chapters five through seven.
Within this moral dimension of discipleship is the distinguishing mark

and central imperative for life which is love (Jn. 15:21-27, I Jn. 4:7-21). Also, one finds humility (Matt. 6:1-18), commitment to God (Matt. 6:22-24), a disciplined life (Matt. 5:19-21, 24), a contentment in God (Phil. 4:10-13), and right treatment for one's fellow Christians (Matt. 7:1-5).[30]

Christ calls his disciples to come together. That is no easy task. It requires the entrance into pain as well as joy with and for other disciples. Douglas Milne looks at discipleship from a biblical basis and indicates that the Gospel of Mark "consistently presents discipleship as a self-denying and costly path of service in imitation of Jesus who came to serve and to give his life as ransom for many (Mark 10:45)."[31] Hinlicky concurs by saying "discipleship in the Gospel of Mark means conforming one's life to Christ,"[32] which is theocentric in nature. Therefore, from the first discipling community that surrounded Jesus to those early resurrection communities and throughout the history of the church, disciples of Christ have attempted to be faithful by coming together one with the other.

Christian disciples must come to their authentic or true self. Though this may seem the strangest dimension of the discipleship journey, it is most important. How does the disciple come to him- or herself? One could suggest that by the very fact of one's existence, one has by definition arrived at being "self-actualized." However, one has not become totally self-actualized until one fulfills the high calling for which God has created us and to which Christ has called us.

> God's plan is to make known his secret to his people, this rich and glorious secret which he has for all peoples. And the secret is that Christ is in you, which means that you will share in the glory of God![33]

One imagines that one's authentic self is in the likeness of Christ. It is not seen at first; rather, it has to be developed in a faithful environment, over a period of time. Through a lifetime of faithfulness, this Christlikeness slowly comes to light as a living witness of the power of God in our lives.

14

Thus, Christ stands at the center of human life, unseen, but present, ready, and waiting to be embodied in the disciple.

> Where does Christ stand? He stands for me. He stands in my place, where I should stand but cannot....Here stands Christ, in the center, between me and myself, between the old existence and the new.[34]

It is then that the disciple comes to his or her authentic, true, or existential self. It is the "self" that C. Eric Lincoln speaks of in his poem, "On Being Myself":

> I want to be the self I want to be,
> the self that lets my inner lights shine through for me,
> the self that lets me be the self I am,
> that leaves me free to swim above the dam.
> I want to be the self that sets me free
> that lets me find the existential me.
> I want to be the self that says to me,
> "Your moment here is your eternity.
> Go kiss a rose; go travel to a star;
> go build a bridge that spans the near and far."
> I want to be the self I'm meant to be:
> the self for which my life was lent to me.[35]

It is then that disciples become "incarnate people" through the likeness of Christ as he matures in their lives. "I live; yet not I, but Christ liveth in me."[36] This likeness of Christ is much more than mere human potential. It is Christ in us who makes our existence purposeful. As the image of Christ unfolds in our lives, so unfolds our calling, our gifts, and our ministry. These spring forth as manifestations of Christ's active presence.

> Those who follow Christ are destined to bear his image, and to be the brethren of the first-born Son of God. Their goal is to become "as Christ." Christ's followers always have his image before their eyes, and in its light all other images are screened from their sight. It penetrates into the depths

15

> of their being, fills them, and makes them more and more like their Master. The image of Jesus Christ impresses itself in daily communion on the image of the disciple. No follower of Jesus can contemplate his image in a spirit of cold detachment. That image has the power to transform our lives, and if we surrender ourselves utterly to him, we cannot help bearing his image ourselves.[37]

"When anyone is joined to Christ, he is a new being; the old is gone, the new has come."[38] "All of us, then, reflect the glory of the Lord with uncovered faces; and that same glory...transforms us into his likeness in an ever greater degree of glory."[39]

Christ is clearly, although not totally, expressed in the person and life of Jesus of Nazareth. The Christ of faith transcends all things and is not restricted to a first-century Jewish male. The Christ of faith is sexless, colorless, and universal, and these qualities allow all people to view and accept Christ as being in their own image, whether they are red, yellow, brown, black, or white. Therefore, Christ can be expressed as female, American, Latin American, African, black, or white. Consequently, God is calling *all* disciples to become what is their most authentic and true self—the fullness of our humanity which is in Christ. When Christ said that a true disciple is one "who comes to me," they are called to come to him, together, one with each other, and to come to their most authentic or true self.

LISTEN

The call of discipleship does not conclude at the command to come. A true disciple is one "who comes to me, and listens to my words." To listen to Christ is no easy task, because Christ speaks in various ways. Sometimes he speaks in ways we rarely expect. Sometimes his voice is easily heard and his commands are easy to follow. Other times, listening to Christ requires a spiritual discipline. Following Christ, as G. K. Chesterton observed, is not always easy: "Christianity has not so much been tried and found wanting, as it has been found difficult and left untried."[40]

Disciples must listen with more than their ears; they must use their hearts, minds, and souls. To listen is to hear the spirit with a spiritual ear that requires a leap of faith, a letting go, a surrender: listening to God's word as he speaks through scripture; listening through our experiences; listening to God in prayer; listening in solitude.

Effective listening is not only obtained by conquering the Bible or by acquiring what it has to offer. Too often when people speak of Bible study, they are seeking to learn *about* the Bible. They attempt to learn about its personalities, message, geography, literary style, etc. They rush into the Bible to glean from it as much as they can. But in so doing, people too often utilize the Bible as a passive book of printed pages, and not the word of life. Acquiring knowledge about the Bible and its contents is an important part of Christian discipleship, but more important is knowledge that leads to Christian growth. The Bible is not merely to be *learned;* rather, it is to be *lived* and *experienced.* Disciples must enter into the Bible stories and become the characters.

For example, when one hears Jesus calling his disciples to cast their nets on the other side, one should be filled with the idea of the "new waters" available to one's life. When one hears of the parable of the two houses, one should question which part of one's life is built upon shaky foundations. When one sees the disciples avoiding the pain of Jesus' impending death by sleeping at Gethsemane, one ought to think of ways of avoiding difficulty and pain. In order to comprehend the teachings of Christ, one must not stand "without" but "within" to understand the meaning of one's life. We, as modern disciples, must enter into the story of the Christian faith and exegetically interpret the text to understand its meaning. Such a task is important to the preaching of the word, to remaining faithful to the word, and to appreciating its message.

OBEY

Jesus said that a true disciple is one "who comes to me, who listens to my words, and obeys them." He proceeds to tell the story of the two houses built with different foundations, as if obedience is the distinguishing factor between the two. The word *obey* means more than keeping a command. How simple discipleship would be if it only required a strict adherence to the Bible in a legalistic sense. But true discipleship is to come, to listen, and to obey in our activity in the world, the Kingdom of God.

To obey means to take the gospel into the world. Discipleship growth can never be expressed through only an internal approach. It is, as Coppedge suggests, a four-step involvement in (a) learning to live under the authority of God, (b) living in fellowship with others who seek to follow God, (c) willingness to trust God and have faith which leads to obedience and love, and (d) having a personal presence of God among his people.[41]

> Discipleship has a twofold intent: the effective proclamation of the Christian gospel to all humanity, making "disciples" from every nation or ethnic group and the development of those disciples' character into the character of Christ himself "teaching them to do all things whatsoever I have commanded you" (Matt. 28:20).[42]

True discipleship is coming to Christ, one with the other, and coming to our most authentic or true self. To obey means to embody Christ in our lives and in the world.

SUMMARY

Discipleship is not an easy task! It came to us through historical roots and evolved over a period of time, and it was Jesus who set the basis of it in the scripture. Discipleship comes after a born-again experience; it is a transformation into a new creation and involves a lifelong process of learning, experiencing, and imaging of Christlikeness. Hence, discipleship is more than mere imitation of the Savior—it is imaging the Christ.

For true discipleship to occur, one must first make an effort to "come" to the Jesus of history and the Christ of faith. When one comes into discipleship, one comes to Jesus Christ, then enters into a lifelong journey with other disciples that ultimately leads to one's true self in Christ. There must be intimacy, accountability, and morality toward other believers, along with a commitment to discipleship. Of course, one must learn to listen or hear the voice of God not only with one's eyes and ears focused on scripture. One must also listen to the lived experiences of life, whether they be within the scripture, history, or one's own life. Finally, answering the call to "come" while "listening" effectively must involve "obedience." To obey means to take the gospel into the world as the embodiment of Christ in our lives and in the world.

Chapter Two:

The Problem of Discipling Black Men

In order to effectively disciple the African American man in today's world, one must first understand him from a historical perspective. Such historical understanding must include an analysis of his social, political, and religious orientation. Culturally he is different from all others, and he brings with him a unique history. He is "American" with the influence of an "African" culture and heritage. Furthermore, his religious practices have been enriched with the overtones of African culture. As the African has been an emotional practitioner of religion, so has the African American male. As white Americans have sought to understand the Christ of faith from a Eurocentric world view, so has the African American male attempted to see Christ in an Afrocentric way as one who identifies with the oppressed.[1]

C. Eric Lincoln cautioned against utilizing European-American ecclesiology as the rule or standard when he eloquently pointed out that

> "Americanity," the prevailing indigenous interpretation of Christianity in America, looks to Western Europe for its ethics and for its supporting values. Behind any spectrum

of value is a cultural history which is the continuing fabric of the social (including the religious) experience of a given society.[2]

The present African American culture has evolved out of a world of frustration, anger, and disillusionment. This began when African American men were enslaved in America after being stolen from their homeland in Africa.

> [During slavery] blacks were defined as a source of organic (or human) property for white slave holders in the notorious "3/5" clause. The clause allowed the slave owner to claim 3/5 constituency for each slave he possessed. Since non-citizens are beyond the pale of legal equality, the Dred Scott decision in 1857 affirmed that slaves were not citizens and could not bring suit in the courts.[3]

From the very beginning of black slavery, African Americans were cut off from their historical roots and culture. White men separated black men from their families as a means of subjugating them: "In the interest of security, every effort was made to separate slaves from a common tribal group or with a common language or religion."[4]

Even during the post-slavery period, blacks felt the consequences of oppression and injustice in the political, social, and economic realms of everyday existence. Yet the black man's religion gave him hope and a sense of being "somebody," both of which in turn gave him his ecclesiology and Christology.

Today, life continues to be difficult for the black man in America. At times, the obstacles seem overwhelming. His problem begins with a high infant mortality rate and a lower life expectancy. For example, although the birth rate of black male and female babies is almost even, by the advent of the young adult years there are fewer black men available in the overall pool.[5] In fact, there are eighteen to twenty-five percent fewer black men than women in the seventeen to forty-five-year-old age group. According to the June issue of *Black Scholar of 1987*, "The great majority of black men will be out of circulation by the year 2000."[6] Many black men will never become active, contributing members of society, in part because of a higher rate of homicide among young black men. Anthony Evans informs us that seventy-two percent of homicide victims are between the ages of eighteen and thirty-nine, and ninety percent of these are black.[7]

Francis Cress Welsing presents a corresponding view:

> We must face the reality that today black men die younger than white men, white women, and black women. Black men are the most frequent victims of homicide, and they are being killed by one another in increasing numbers. The suicide rate for young black men is the only black suicide rate greater than the rates of whites....Black infant mortality remains two to three times the figure for whites. We continue to have the highest rates of separation and divorce, thus, family dissolution. We continue to have some of the highest rates of teenage parenthood....We continue to have high levels of juvenile delinquency, gang wars, and drug addiction.[8]

A radio commentator once painted the following picture:

> A black juvenile male is four times more likely than his white counterpart to be incarcerated for a violent offense. Only twelve percent of the nation's young male population is black. Yet, mainly because of intravenous drug use, African Americans account for one third of AIDS cases for that group. One out of every four black men is under court control, either in jail, on parole, or on probation. For young black men the leading cause of death is murder. The mood on the street is fatalistic....Black men are much more likely to die of diseases ranging from hypertension to lung cancer. A study just released shows nearly one third of the black Americans who died in 1987 would have survived if they had lived under the same health conditions as whites. Black males are often not active participants in the rearing of their children; in fact, over half of all black homes are headed by a single female parent, and the vast majority live

at or below the poverty line. Also, so many black men grow up with fathers they never really know.[9]

Today, fewer black men are in college than in prison.[10] In fact, studies frequently correlate these high incarceration rates with low education rates. Henry C. Gregory III reports the following 1990 statistics in Washington, D.C. alone:

> Of the prison population in the District of Columbia, 91% are black males and 5.9% are black females. The largest crime category is drug offenses, making up 44.4%. Violent crimes now account for 30% and property crimes rank third with 11.6%. The drug offenses have increased 5% in the last year. The marital status is 80.4% single, 12.8% married, and the remaining persons separated or divorced. In terms of the educational level of inmates, 50.6% completed grades seven to eleven; 38.1% claimed high school completion; and 2.2% have lower than seventh grade education. The remaining 9.1% had some college or other training beyond high school.[11]

Acquiring inadequate education severely restricts the ability of young black men to obtain employment and develop careers to support themselves and their families. As Haki R. Madhubuti points out:

> Less than half of the black students in the high school class of 1990 will finish; and of those who do, most will be uneducated. With the unemployment rate for black males approaching forty-eight percent, the future does not look too inviting. Less than four percent of the jobs in the United States are manned by black men.[12]

Furthermore, the Bureau of Labor Statistics reported in 1988 that "fifty-eight percent of all future jobs will require four years of high school and one to two years of college."[13] But because the high school dropout rate is extremely high for black males, many of them are shut out of the job market in the U.S. and are forced to seek employment

24

elsewhere. Even if black men educate themselves and attempt to enter the American work force, they are still at an economic disadvantage. John E. Jacobs, president and chief executive officer of the National Urban League, states that "for black men, it will take seventy-three years at the current rate of progress to close the racial gap in earnings."[14]

Clearly, even before African American males reach adulthood, they are faced with many seemingly insurmountable obstacles. It is perhaps understandable why some black males, faced with these difficulties, turn to crime as a matter of sheer survival.

> Crime, economic deprivation and masculinity are all intertwined....Even when a strong economic need is absent, black men may gravitate toward criminality in order to achieve cultural goals that are established for all members of the society. The masculine ethic of success leads them to commit illegal acts when the dominant culture restricts access to socially accepted ways of attaining those goals. Colonialism creates a feeling of alienation when the black male senses that he is not part of the society, that he is powerless to determine his life chances. In such a situation, the only law that is relevant to him is the law of survival.[15]

In the United States, the African American man is virtually powerless, landless, and moneyless in a society that measures manhood by such acquisition. When he cannot provide himself or his family with the "American dream" through legitimate means, he often turns to crime in order to attain that dream. As a result, the black male prison population is over fifty percent nationwide.[16]

The problems of the African American male and the black family are reflected in the black church. For the reasons described above, black men are often no longer free to attend church. But even when men are able to join and attend church, they often refuse to do so because of "cultural reasoning." For example, many men believe that church is something for women and children only.[17] Indeed, it is easy to surmise that church is for women and children when one sees that it is mostly women and children who attend church in the first place. C. Eric Lincoln and Lawrence H. Mamiya write that

> any casual observer of a Sunday worship service in the typical black church is immediately struck by the predominance of female members. Depending on the congregation, between sixty-six and eighty percent of its membership is usually composed of women. In our survey of 2,150 churches, male membership averaged thirty percent. There are about 2.5 to 3 females to every male member. The usual anguished lament and question heard from pastor and laity are, "Where have all the black men gone? Why don't more black men attend church?"[18]

McLain further asserts that

> by the next decade, manpower in the black church will have dwindled even more. There may be, by the year 2000, thirty to forty women to every man in the church. If this trend continues to go unchallenged and unchecked, the young black churchman will dwindle and women will be called upon to lead. Most of the churches in America are now being carried by women.[19]

Clearly, this lack of men in the black church must be addressed. Too often the church is slow in expressing concern regarding this decline at the local level. The truth of the matter is, as McLain says, "on the whole, church membership has less meaning for modern man. There are exceptions of course, but most men who have joined the church have weak ties to it, and those who have not joined are too often unimpressed by it."[20]

The Bible clearly speaks of the need for the discipleship of all persons.[21] It is not enough for people to be saved; they also need to be taught.[22] Since black men are not actively attending church or are not involved in ministry, it becomes the responsibility of the church to address this problem.

In researching what should be done to bring men into church,

McLain discovered several reasons for the lack of male presence in many congregations. Interviews with young black men ages eighteen to thirty-one who were brought up in the church but were not currently active reveal several reasons why they stopped attending:

1) The church was no longer relevant to their everyday lives.
2) The church did not address the sexual revolution or equip young people with a survival kit and the knowledge to withstand the pressures of the world.
3) Other than repeating "Just Say No," the church remains ignorant and silent regarding the drug crisis.
4) The church has not translated the New Testament message to address contemporary problems.
5) For those former members who are hanging out there, trapped in the world, the church's hands do not reach outside its doors.
6) Young men and women are caught in an endless cycle of social fast lanes and economic dead ends.
7) After leaving the church to experience the world, if one does make it back, oftentimes he or she is too burned out, hung over, spaced out, or run down to be of any immediate use.[23]

To this list, Edward P. Wimberly adds the following:

> Another significant concern is religion, which becomes dominant around the transition age of thirty, when young adulthood is coming to an end. The adult is settling down, and part of settling down is giving attention to the role one will play in the faith drama story. Concern for one's spiritual roots is present during young adulthood, but the transition age of thirty, generally accompanied by full launching into the world, stimulates the need to give attention to one's spiritual basis.[24]

In other words, Wimberly is suggesting that African Americans are generally not interested in religion until they reach the transitional age of thirty. Those experiencing young adulthood are too busy "finding themselves." They are attending college, starting families, and setting out on their career ventures.

There are also sociological factors hindering not only black men but also black people as a whole from attending inner-city churches. In *The Black Male: The New Bald Eagle*, Jeffrey M. Johnson observes the following:

> A recent *Washington Post* article on the black church high-lighted some of the reasons for church membership declines. They included blacks moving from the city to the suburbs, the fact that blacks under the age of thirty are a vanishing breed of church-goers, a general lack of interest in the church, and a perception that the church lacks the commitment to deal with today's social problems, including teen pregnancy, drugs, and AIDS.[25]

Gwendolyn Rice adds that "many of the men who are unchurched might consider being a part of our churches were they to see the church involved in significant community outreach."[26]

SUMMARY

Discipling black men in today's world is extremely difficult when one considers the world of the African American male. First of all, his world is literally short-lived. His infant mortality rate is higher than that of his non-black counterparts. His life expectancy rate is also the lowest of anyone's. Death is ever present in his high rate of homicide, suicide, and health-related problems. Due to his lack of education and his economic degradation, he finds himself turning to crime for the sake of survival, sustenance, and mental health. Hence, the black male constitutes the highest percent of the prison population nationwide. Subsequently, discipling the black male is extremely difficult, in part because the church has so few available to disciple.

To disciple the pool of available men, the church must first overcome a number of difficulties. One problem is countering the myth that church is for women and children. Some studies suggest that the church might overcome this perception by becoming more involved in the social concerns and contemporary problems of black men. In this way, churches could present a religion that is more relevant to men in their everyday lives. Another difficulty the church must overcome is the fact that while many men whom the church would most benefit live in the inner city, many churches have recently relocated to the suburbs. Clearly, these and a host of other problems contribute to the difficulty of discipling black males in today's world.

Chapter Three:

Contemporary Models

In order to disciple black men, we must first realize and understand the many problems the African American faces in this country. If these men are going to be reached, they must be understood culturally, sociologically, and economically, as well as demographically. Knowing this information can enhance our understanding of why they are not being discipled. To reach them, we must become sensitive to their plight. They in turn need to know that their history did not begin in America. Francis Cress Welsing writes:

> There is a proverb that states, "The tree grows strong and tall only to the extent that its roots are deep and firmly planted in the soil." If black people are at all disappointed in our present level of achievement, it may be because our roots are not planted deeply enough in the past—resting upon shallow, inadequate, and faulty data input of only four hundred years of history.[1]

Black men must learn their history so that they can define themselves. As Carroll Felton, Jr. points out, "A major concern among an oppressed people is that of self-identity: the basic question of 'Who am

I?' which initiates the definitional process is highly significant."[2]
George Santayana, the American philosopher, adds, "Those who do
not know their history and do not learn from history will repeat it."[3]
In addition, the black man must not only learn his historical roots, but
he must also tackle the question of his purpose. Unquestionably, the
black man searches for meaning in a three-dimensional way: "He is
concerned about where he came from, where he is going, and the
meaning of his existence here and now."[4] Furthermore, the black man
is highly motivated to explore this multidimensional facet of his being.

> If you do not know who you were, it is likely you do not
> know where you are going. And if you do not know where
> you are going, any old fool can take you there, and once
> you arrive you still will be lost and neither history nor your
> children will forgive you for being lost.[5]

For the black man, history includes not only the past but the present
as well as the future. If we wish to disciple him, it is in our interest to
aid him in this mission of self-discovery.

A thorough knowledge of one's history can potentially lead to an
appreciation of one's culture, which in turn plays an important role in
developing one's Christology and theology.

> There is not one Christian theology, but many Christian
> theologies which are valid expressions of the gospel of
> Jesus....It depends on race, sex, class, and situation. It takes
> into account social and political situation.[6]

Black men are willing to accept a theology that takes into account
their particular experiences. That theology then points to the practices
and processes that should be involved in their discipleship. Therefore,
it becomes important that black men are not "deculturated" from
their blackness or "acculturated" to whiteness.[7] Black theology, unlike
traditional theology, leads to the creation and practice of a black theology of liberation, through which black men are able to see how
"God was in Christ reconciling the world unto himself."[8] It is easy to

see why black men would be drawn to a Christ of faith who identifies with their predicaments.

Like everyone, black men must hear the gospel message that leads to discipleship. Once those men hear the message and repent of their sins, they can then begin—as Philippians 2:12 suggests—to work out their salvation by being delivered from the power of sin. They, too, can come to Christ, one with the other, and to their most authentic self. They, too, can then listen and obey by making Christ real in their lives and in the world.

These men can also be discipled on a one-to-one basis. Men can bring men to church and then hold each other accountable for their Christian walk and commitment. This accountability can incorporate intimacy, which leads to cooperation, rather than coercion, along one's journey of Christian discipleship.

Christian discipleship grows and develops over a long period of time. Learning to live under the authority of God, and in fellowship with others who seek to follow God, is a lifelong journey. It took Jesus three full years to train the twelve disciples.[9] Clearly, it will take more than a lecture or a workshop on Christian discipleship to produce true disciples. Jesus continuously shared his life with the twelve, guiding them, loving them, correcting them, encouraging them, forgiving them, and praying for them. Therefore, in order to disciple black men today, we must realize that no short-term course will do the job.

Discipleship is more than superficially imitating Jesus Christ; it involves modeling. Men must model themselves after other Christian men. "Through the men in whom Jesus had poured his life, his word and life were made known to other men. The Christian's responsibility and greatest honor is to make Christ known to other men."[10] The church must develop mentoring ministries for men as well as small group discipling programs. In addition, we must institute Bible classes for men, along with male chorus meetings, men's fellowship and prayer groups, men's evangelistic teams, deaconship programs, and the like.

The African American man must be equipped for his task and mission, and the church must become the place where this training takes place. The pastor becomes key to the discipleship process and must obtain the theological skills needed for the job. Furthermore, when the black pastor becomes the expert at equipping the men for ministry, he must also present himself as a person of integrity, avoiding and dispelling even the perception of character flaws. For example:

> The black church image of the black minister has been maintained as a sexual man. Because of his high status in the black community, it was natural that many black women would find sexual appeal in his prestigious status, his command of oratory, his wealth, and flamboyance....Also, as Hernton comments, the common songs, myths, jokes, and ditties about the sexual activity of the black preacher [are legendary].[11]

As a result, the black preacher is given the awesome task of dispelling such myths. For a myth to have impact, it need only be believed. Belief in a myth is based to a large degree upon the thoughts, feelings, and words that send it forth.

SELECTED CONTEMPORARY MODELS

There are few black churches in this country that have active programs seeking to disciple black males. They are (1) Trinity United Church of Christ, Chicago, Illinois; (2) Oak Cliff Bible Fellowship, Oak Cliff, Texas; (3) St. Paul Community Baptist Church, Brooklyn, New York; and (4) Concord Missionary Baptist Church, Dallas, Texas. In addition to these four models, Haki R. Madhubuti, author of Black Men: *Obsolete, Single, Dangerous?*,[12] along with Jawanza Kunjufu, who has written several books on black males, offers insightful suggestions when dealing with the African American male.

What follows is an examination of each of the four models, with an assessment of the strengths and weaknesses of each. My assessments of these models, combined with my own personal research, will provide a comprehensive model for the discipling of black men.

When I began my study, none of the aforementioned churches

had written documentation of their models, other than the Reverend Johnny Youngblood, pastor of the St. Paul Community Baptist Church. His documentation was in the form of his Doctor of Ministry project, entitled *The Black Male in the Local Church.* Because of the shortage of documentation, most of the information gathered and presented here was acquired through interviews.

The Trinity United Church of Christ in Chicago, Illinois, pastored by Jeremiah A. Wright, Jr., has a total membership of 5,000 people, with an active membership of 2,500 to 3,000. Wright was happy to inform me that during any given Sunday service, thirty to forty percent of his congregation consists of men. His church is known throughout the country and among leading pastors for its growing black male ministry.

Jeremiah Wright became interested in the plight of African American men when he was challenged to deal with inner-city black males. A leading scholar had informed him that most black churches appeal primarily to middle class, highly influential black men, while the lower class, unemployed, streetwise male was being overlooked. Wright believed that the Black Muslims were the main group in America attempting to convert these men; it was the Muslims who entered the jails and prisons to evangelize these men.

This challenge motivated Wright to minister to *all* black males. He began by announcing from the pulpit his burden and concern for the African American male. After he had shared his concern, he announced several Sundays in advance that he would meet with all men—churched or unchurched, sick or poor, educated or uneducated. He met with them for an hour each Saturday afternoon, lecturing on the writings of black authors like Jawanza Kunjufu and Naim Akbar and conducting Bible studies. The men responded immediately to Wright's Afrocentric perspective. He discovered that they were most interested in learning about their historical roots and about the issues facing today's black man. He presented basic Bible principles to enable them to deal with their problems as black men, and as a result, they wanted to take action, to organize and design further programs to reinforce what they had learned in the group. They organized an Adult Male Mentoring Program to further develop positive male role models. They also assembled small cell groups for prayer, fellowship, and Bible studies. Furthermore, they instituted an early morning Sunday service for men who wanted to come to church early.

Wright uses an informal approach in discipling black males. He gathers the men in the sanctuary and lectures to them each Saturday. During the week, they are broken down into cell groups where they are given specific instructions regarding Bible study. Both the lecture and group meetings include discussion time, as well as a question and answer period. The men in the new members class must make a commitment to serve in some ministry, which is followed up by the pastor and an auxiliary representative. In addition, Wright instituted an accountability system to keep each member of the group from failing in his commitment and to ensure his presence in Sunday worship and ministry.

Wright thinks that men are attracted to his church because he presents a positive role model for them and offers a unique presentation that makes the Bible come alive through their experiences. He noted that his lecture series on male-female relationships was probably the most appreciated.

> The most-liked lecture series dealt with "what does it mean to be the head of your household?" The issue of how to love a woman and be a man was well received. The men enjoyed learning the role of the woman as a partner where she is not subordinated in terms of being inferior....She maintains her personality in being made in the image of God, [in] being a co-creator.[13]

Not only does Wright attempt to make the Bible come alive to the men, but he does so in common terms. In other words, he does not attempt to use standard English but instead speaks to them in their own dialect—black English.

Those men with Ph.D.s talk the same language as those on
A.D.C. [meaning county welfare recipients]. African Americans are a bilingual people. We adjust our conversational
dialect to the setting [in which] we find ourselves. Therefore, I approach all brothers in the same way.[14]

Finally, Wright sees his model as one that attempts to clarify values for black men. He believes that black men have acquired a value
system that is in need of constant clarification. For example, black
men, he believes, have been taught the wrong use of their sexuality.
They need to be taught the rightful role of sexual relationships within
the confines of God's regulations.

This model seems to be a good start, in the sense that the pastor
must have an initial concern for men and a need to express this concern from the pulpit. Furthermore, his development of "cell groups"
is excellent for maintaining some type of accountability system. The
new member class is certainly a positive reinforcement, because it
gains a commitment from new men as they enter the church membership. In addition, Wright's use of black dialect increases his ability
to relate to African American men, because it allows the less educated
male to more easily identify with his message.

Oak Cliff Bible Fellowship of Texas is also an excellent model of
male discipling. It is pastored by the Reverend Anthony Evans, who has
an active membership of about 2,500. The adult male membership and
Sunday attendance is about forty percent. One does not merely join this
church by stepping forward on a Sunday morning. One must enter an
exhaustive new membership class, sign a covenantal agreement that
includes one's concurrence not to legally sue the church, be active in at
least one ministry, and give financially to the church, along with other
agreed upon stipulations. Although these requirement may seem a little
extreme, the church has a national following. It offers marriage workshops, male seminars, books on the family, and many other services.
Evans attributes his large adult male following to expository preaching.
He is of the opinion that such sermons do the converting and discipling

of males. Evans has not thought through a specific male discipling program, but he does have a model for the church that includes a stringent accountability system, positive male role models, morality in the home, and a check-and-balance system for leaders in the church. The expectation of church membership is not based on a verbal agreement but on a signed covenantal contract. The strength of such a written contract is that the members, male and female, can be held accountable to their contracts. This can be an excellent reinforcer of one's commitment because discipleship is spelled out in concrete terms.

The church has a manual on the meaning of the church and Christian discipleship that is taught prior to becoming a new member. A new member also completes a questionnaire to test his recollection of biblical principles. Evans meets monthly with his leaders to hold them accountable for the membership and their discipleship journey. In this way, Oak Cliff Bible Fellowship takes a holistic approach to discipleship. For Evans, discipleship is not to be addressed to any one particular group in the church, but to all who are Christians.

St. Paul Community Baptist Church of Brooklyn, New York, is pastored by the Reverend Johnny Youngblood. Youngblood has a membership of 6,000 people, with an active membership of about 2,800. He holds two Sunday morning worship services, each of which is about twenty percent male.

Youngblood's male discipling model is aimed at the streetwise, lower income, adult black male. St. Paul is situated on the Brooklyn and Queens border. As Wright and Evans did in their models, Youngblood made an appeal from the pulpit, sharing his concern and sadness at the lack of men in the church. He invited the congregation to bring men to the church, and informed them that he intended "to win men to Christ." After giving a special invitation in Sunday service, Youngblood began holding Bible classes for men during the Sunday school hour. Initially, twenty-five to forty men attended the class. Later, the Bible class was extended to a week night, during which Youngblood allowed the men to openly discuss any subject they desired. They dealt with male-female relationships, racism, economics, drugs, sexuality, and other relevant issues. Youngblood attempted to create a trusting environment by using black dialect; he found that the men could more easily identify with him when he both used and allowed derogatory terms in class. Youngblood referred to the characters of Peter and David to make the Bible text come alive. For Youngblood, Peter was a good example because he was a rough and rugged fisherman by trade, carried a knife, and used derogatory terms and expressions. David, on the other hand, was famous for his bravery and his love of women. The class was extremely interested in identifying with such "human" characters, as well as with blacks in the Bible. For these men, a Eurocentric Christ or, as Youngblood puts it, "an Americanized Christ," is unacceptable to black men. Youngblood utilized the writings of Jawanza Kunjufu and Naim Akbar and attempted to intertwine the black cultural and sociological aspects of these writings with biblical principles. Through his experiences, he discovered that it is the study of Afrocentricity which most often attracts men to church, but it is the Bible that keeps them there. For that reason, Youngblood later created a class that dealt strictly with the Bible.

During the year, St. Paul holds two worship services geared for men only. Women and children of the congregation are prohibited from attending these services, which are geared toward inspiring men to become closer to God. From these services, the church developed an all-male chorus, a "Sons of David" group in which the experiences of young David (who had to fight a lion, a bear, and a giant) are compared to those obstacles the men must face and overcome.

Youngblood has incorporated no real accountability system into this model. Basically, the pastor holds each man accountable for his presence as an active member of the church. It is the pastor who directs the ministry and calls men to a point of accountability both collectively and individually.

Youngblood's approach results in some interesting insights into a group of men who are not being reached in the black church—specifically inner-city, streetwise black men. He believes that the following problems keep men out of the church: (a) an outright misunderstanding of Christianity or an overreaction to American Christianity, which does not deal with the plight of African American men; (b) a perception by men that the church is an institution for women and children; (c) the women's perception of the preacher (black women often create a kind of rivalry between their allegiance to their spouse and to their pastor); and (d) the perpetuation of a feminized version of Christianity.

The final model that we shall consider is one developed by the Reverend E. K. Bailey of the Concord Missionary Baptist Church in Dallas, Texas. His church is located in a lower middle class, inner city area, but the majority of his worshippers come from the suburbs. Although Bailey's model had not been written or published when I was conducting my original research, it was certainly well thought out. He described the church's membership as follows:

> There is a "brag" number, and that's the number most preachers want to brag about. It's the number on roll, and God knows when I get to heaven I won't be able to account for all of those. These are those who call themselves members of Concord. I have a "brag number" of about 5,000 members. And then I have what I call the average Sunday morning attendees, which averages about 1,700 to 2,300. That sounds more like my active membership. We have really about seven hundred to eight hundred core families.[15]

At that time, Bailey had an average of thirty to forty percent adult black male attendees at Sunday services. However, Bailey told me that he has a personal goal of fifty percent adult black male Sunday morning worshippers.

When asked if he believes there is an overall absence of black adult males in the church, Bailey responded,

> Yes, even broader than that; all races of people are having trouble getting men in the church. In the African American community, we are at the bottom of the totem pole on all these issues, and it is no exception when it comes to the African American church.[16]

Bailey thinks that black men do not come to church because they believe the church does not address their social, political, or economic needs. He further suggested that black men do not appreciate the pastor's misuse of power:

> Black men view the black preacher as being extremely powerful in the black church. They see the black preacher as an extension of an already oppressive society in that he too has absolute authority. To black men, black preachers operate on the basis of power that corrupts. It causes them to be intimidated by the power that they see invested in this one individual....If a leader is not aware of this perception and not wise enough to organize a shared leadership, then he will not be able to attract men.
>
> Leaders are not transparent enough to build and invest their confidence in this individual. Transparency is a key to helping black men. The sin issue has a lot to do with it. In Genesis 3, God cursed everybody who participated in bringing sin into the world. And what it did to woman was totally different from what it did to the man. It caused the man to abdicate his leadership responsibilities. God had called the man to be the leader, and the man, because of sin, relinquished that responsibility and allowed woman to assume it.
>
> What you have is the man not wanting to lead in general. Women have assumed that responsibility in a lot of areas. God had invested a special kind of intuition to women, which allows women to be more sensitive to spiritual things. Hence, you have to work harder to get men to recognize and appreciate spiritual things because of his intuition.[17]

Bailey's model begins in a similar fashion to the other three models. There is first a concern for men on the part of the pastor. Bailey expands this concern to utilize the term "vision." He suggests that there must be a vision for men in the church:

> A pastor must have a vision for his church. Without a vision the people perish. The secular world operates around

41

visions. But not the local church....Men represent the strength of a race, the strength of a church. Therefore, in order to have a strong church, you have to have strong families. The preacher must be concerned about rebuilding the infrastructure of the African American family. The family is the cornerstone of any race of people. One of the keys to building this infrastructure is the man.

One must care about the church, care about the family, and care [about] men. One must present ministries designed to equip and empower the African American male. Then one begins to have a vision for men....Once that vision is understood, then one must develop a ministry model to make the vision come alive.[18]

Bailey's model has three parts: (a) a vision for attracting men, (b) a discipleship component, and (c) an accountability component. He suggests that to begin a male discipleship program, one must first pray for a vision for such a model. For Bailey, prayer is essential to seeking the will of God for the direction of both the church and pastor, as well as the men. He suggests a prayer vigil, for which the church members gather to pray for the adult male population. Second, an all-male workshop, seminar, retreat, or breakfast meeting should be held to discuss the problems that men have. He believes that young boys could be invited to such a meeting, because the survival of the men includes the survival of the boys. During this initial stage, a discussion of biblical concepts of manhood and the problems of racism, economic development, and family issues could be the focus of attention. From these meetings, a vision for discipling black men could evolve that would entail an all-inclusive model of the recommendations and suggestions of the participants.

When creating the vision, pastors need to give motivational sermons and lectures on the importance of the family. Bailey suggested that guest lecturers be brought in to discuss key issues regarding the black family structure both from a historical and contextual point of view. Marital enrichment seminars would also be included within this component of the model to strengthen the bond between men and women. A separate ministry seminar would be helpful in dealing with the single men. Bailey recommended that these workshops, seminars, and retreats be highly structured, with a formal educational approach that would include textbooks, required readings, and possibly even quizzes. The rationale is that formal training will produce men who may want to read and further their spiritual development in a formal way.

The second component is the discipling process. This would be a church-wide program, or one that dealt not only with discipling black men but discipling the family as well. Bailey suggested that prior to being accepted into this particular program, men would be screened to determine their level of commitment. They would be men who were "F.A.T.": faithful, available, and teachable.

Bailey believes that the first component of his model would help those who merely want to talk about their problems and receive some guidance in resolving them. The second level, however, would be made available for those who want to do something more than talk about the problem. This group would include men who have shown faithfulness to the church and to Bible study. These would be men who made themselves eligible through their attendance at church and at meetings. The participants at this level would have exhibited some degree of humility through their willingness to be taught by others. For Bailey, these men would become the future leaders in the church.

Bailey explained that men who have reached this level could become home Bible study leaders. One of the prerequisites would be that they must open their homes weekly for Bible study groups with their fellow male church members.

> The church started in the home, so it's just going back where it started—it's going home! When a man lets you into his home, he is letting his guard down. Spiritually it is the equivalent of letting up a hood and letting the mechanic get under there to find out what's wrong. When a man allows you to come into his domicile, his place where he is king, in his heart he is beginning to open up for you to begin the developmental process. Men bond together as

brothers in the home more so than when meeting upon neutral grounds such as the church.[19]

Bailey believes that light refreshments, not expensive dinners, should be served at these meetings. Teaching should be organized, timely, consistent, and should provide a role model—"Remember that whatever you project as a model may be duplicated in the student."

During this period, men must also attend a weekly two-hour, open Bible class. The first hour consists of a pastoral lecture and a question and answer period. The second hour would include prayer, testimonials, time for sharing, and fellowship, which includes refreshments. Also, women are encouraged to join the group during the second hour.

The third component of this model deals with the question of accountability. For Bailey, accountability is very important in the role of discipling men. Those men who stay at level one are not held accountable for their commitment. Those who desire leadership roles and enter level two, however, are held accountable for their discipleship commitment. Bailey believes that there is true growth when there is accountability.

All leaders are required to attend the pastor's annual church growth seminar, workshops, and the annual African American Male Seminar, which consists mostly of lectures from guest speakers.

Bailey's model for discipling black males distinguishes between those who want to remain nominal Christians versus those who want to embark upon the total journey of discipleship. The two levels of commitment enable the individual to decide on his level of involvement, a choice which helps to create a non-threatening, quite acceptable model.

Evaluation of All Four Models

As I reflected on all the models, I recognized that Youngblood's and Wright's models have a particular appeal to the inner city, low-to-middle-class, streetwise male. These pastors relate to their men using street language and attempt to reach out to them personally—to view them in light of their particular struggles. Of course, this is easier for Youngblood and Wright, whose churches are located in the inner city, while Evans' and Bailey's churches are either in a suburb or bordering one. Furthermore, Youngblood's and Wright's models include substantial black cultural material, and they both utilize Kunjufu's and Akbar's materials. In contrast, Evans and Bailey incorporated little cultural material in their models, which were chiefly based on expository preaching and included more Bible studies than did Youngblood's or Wright's.

Despite these basic differences, all four models deal with family issues, male and female relationships, and the manhood of black men. Three of the models, however (those of Youngblood, Wright, and Bailey), attempt to push men's programs to the exclusion of other church programs. Therefore, when conducting my research, it seemed appropriate to consider a woman's view of such a model, since women are ultimately affected by the impact of the discipling of black men, which in turn impacts their daily lives and relationships. I contacted Kelly Brown of Howard University in Washington, D.C. to ask for her input on developing a discipling program for black men. She acknowledged the absence of black males in the church today:

> According to C. Eric Lincoln's book, *The Black Church in the African American Experience*, the black church is overwhelmingly female, seventy-five percent women in the average black church, [a rate] which is higher than [that of] white churches....Also, the majority of leadership in the black church is male. However, religion has always been thought to be the domain of the woman. That's been the patriarchal stereotype. Black people feed into that.[20]

She goes on to suggest that when one considers the absence of black men in church, one must consider the overall demographics of African Americans. In other words, it is difficult to get black men into church when there are so few black males in circulation today.

45

Brown's suggestions for creating a discipling program for black males included an understanding of the demographics of black men. She feels that such a model needs to focus even more on the problems faced by African American men. She stated that

> we are losing them at a disproportionate and alarming [rate]. We have to focus in on issues of self-esteem, issues of teaching African American children about their culture and history. We must make the church relevant to where they are and who they are.[21]

Most importantly, Brown argued that such a model must not merely focus on the problems faced by men. In other words, to focus on the problems of the males without also discussing the family would be to the detriment of all African Americans. Brown suggested that to help the black male, one must create a model that helps the entire family, because the breakdown of the woman is also a contributing factor to the breakdown of the man. Brown points out that

> traditionally—historically, the female has been the one to rear the children, the purveyor of sustaining the culture and values of our children. What we now see is what happens when the female is absent. Historically, the black male has been absent. That has been the case since slavery, not because he has wanted to be absent, but oppressive forces have made that the case. What's new? Why is the black family as we have known it suddenly disintegrating? Why are the children suddenly at risk? Why are all these black males suddenly at risk? I suggest that it has something to do with the black female. She, too, is now absent.[22]

Brown suggested that in order to help the black male, we must also attempt to help black females and children. Therefore, a ministry model must help the whole family, because black women and their children can be instrumental in bringing the black men into the church. Brown added that such a model must include ministry to the entire community and recommended that the church needs to promote programs during the week as diligently as we do Bible studies and all those other things which are important, which we consider nontraditional functions of the church. Somehow, we've got to get over this sacred/secular split—that certain things don't belong in the church. Everything that has to do with the survival and well-being of our community belongs in the church.[23]

Brown concluded our discussion by asserting that any model of discipling black men exclusive of the rest of the black family would be detrimental to the entire African American community.

I think the church should promote a model that includes the family, the community. There are particulars that relate to men that have to be addressed, and there are particular issues that relate to women that have to be addressed. So the issue here is not to promote men, or to promote women, but to promote the survival of the family, of the community. I don't think we need to get that out of balance.[24]

Part Two:

A Discipling Program

Chapter Four:

How to Begin

The Bible says, "Where there is no vision, the people perish."[1] In order to begin a discipling program for African American men, one must first have a desire to bring men into the church. Reverend E. K. Bailey calls this a "burden that leads to a vision."[2] One must feel a deep need to bring men into the church, an inner urge and desire to face the problem. Some pastors are driven to bring men into the church because they observe their absence and the lack of male participation in the service. Others may be motivated by a deep yearning to have those of their own gender actively involved in the mission of the church to "reconcile the world back to God."[3] Then there may be those who recognize what a difference God can make in the everyday lives of African American men and their families, who are often faced with oppression, racism, and discrimination.

Reverend Jeremiah Wright, for example, was challenged by a friend to begin discipling inner city men. It was then that he developed a true desire to bring men to Christ and disciple them for service. Reverend Johnny Youngblood, on the other hand, grew concerned at the small number of men in his church when he conducted a reassessment of his

ministry. Though his congregation had grown numerically and economically and the church was well off, Youngblood was unhappy at
the noticeable lack of men. He felt as John had, on the lonely island
of Patmos—"Shipwrecked unto himself." Though he was pleased at
the participation of the women, children, and youth, he found that he
missed the presence of those of his own gender. Once he acknowledged the need for more men in the church, he began to actively seek
their involvement in the ministry.

A Call for Men

Once a pastor decides to set up a special ministry for men, there are
several methods he can use to get men into church.

1. The Andrew method. This is the method of personal evangelism
utilized by Andrew, Simon Peter's brother. The record of his work is
found in John 1:40, 41: "One of the two which heard John speak, and
followed him [Christ], was Andrew, Simon's brother. He first findeth
his own brother Simon, and saith unto him, we have found the Mes-
sias, which is being interpreted, the Christ."4 The pastor can thus
invite men individually to the church, or he may extend a personal
invitation to the membership to bring men to church. As men begin
to attend the church, the pastor can follow up their visit by sending
them a letter, calling them, or visiting them at home. Also, the pastor
may encourage the men by acknowledging their presence during worship services.

2. Two-by-two visitation. This is the modern adaptation of the
method Jesus used when sending his disciples out into the world to
deliver his message to others. One proclaims the good news, and the
other bears witness to the proclamation. After the pastor has expressed
his concern for the lack of male church members, he can challenge the
entire congregation to bring men into the church and encourage the
men to invite other men to church.

3. Deputation teams. This is the method of grouping men in twos,
threes, or even fours and training them to speak on a specific topic

before the general congregation and other men's groups. These teams study different areas of concentration together. They work out their talks together and are sent out together to give their message to unreached and unchurched men. Through this third method, groups of men can work together to reach other men and bring them into the church. The advantage in creating such groups is that a core group of men evolves and grows in their own discipleship as they work to disciple other men.

A MEETING

The pastor's next step is to announce a meeting of all men ages eighteen and over, both in and out of the church. This public announcement should be followed by a letter from the pastor to all men of the church.

The pastor should pay special attention to the setting of the first meeting. It should take place in an informal setting where the men can feel free to express themselves. Perhaps it would be best to seat the men in a circle, where they each can observe the facial expressions and body language of the others. This form of non-verbal communication is crucial to good group dynamics.

Most pastors believe that they must wear a white shirt and tie to all meetings. However, my experience has been that black men are less intimidated when the pastor attends the men's meeting wearing less formal attire. I have dressed causally for many of these informal sessions, and many of the men have told me that they appreciate my relaxed appearance; they felt more comfortable because I had come "dressed for the occasion."

During this initial meeting, the pastor should encourage a discussion period with plenty of time for questions and answers. Men need to talk! Black men have sometimes been penalized for speaking their minds, but everyone has a right to his opinion, and this should be a time in which everyone can be heard. Above all, the discussion should center on the plight of African American men.

TOPICS	DISCUSSION SUGGESTIONS
Racism	Discrimination on the job; unfair hiring and firing practices; unequal pay for equal work; discrimination in promotion practices; discrimination in housing and in acquiring home loans
Drugs	Drugs being sold in the black community; drugs as a billion dollar industry in America; drugs killing families; babies being born addicted to crack; what has happened to the war on drugs? Where are the treatment programs? How much of the government's money to fight drugs has actually reached black people?
Identity crises	Why do blacks not know who they are? Why do blacks need to know where they have come from historically? What is the importance of knowing their African and slavery heritage? What are the results of not knowing who you are? Why are there so many different names for black people? What makes black people different from other people? Why do some blacks hate themselves?
Education	Why is it important to get a good education? Why go to an all-black

Topics	Discussion suggestions
	college? Why was there court-ordered busing? Was it good or bad? Why are there more black men in prison than in college?
Black men	Where are the men? Are they in jail, on drugs, unemployed or underemployed, out in the world finding themselves? Do they die at a higher rate than their white counterparts? Why are homicide rates so high for black males in America? Are there so many single-parent homes because black men are irresponsible and don't want to take care of their families? Why do black male babies die at such a high rate?
Communication	What are some popular black movies today? How do they portray the black man? What are the lyrics to popular songs that our youth listen to, and how do those lyrics affect them? How are black males depicted on television? What are their roles? Why should men listen to the news and read the newspaper? Should black men speak only standard English versus black English?

Topics	Discussion suggestions
Family	Is your family important? How much time do you spend with your children and your wife? Why do so many black marriages end in divorce or remain unstable? How much time do your children spend watching T.V.? Do you have Bible study with your family? What were the dynamics of the African family? What are the roles of the father, mother, and children in today's African American family?

Chapter Five:

Meeting the Challenge

SELF-DEVELOPMENT

If we accept the premise that the black male is endangered, we must then determine what can be done to preserve him. The church must provide support by developing a plan of attack to ensure the black man's survival, and pastors must plan and coordinate these efforts using every available resource.

Restoring the African American male to dignity and to his rightful place within the church, family, and state must include self-development for each man. This process begins when the man redefines himself by first dealing with his culture and history. He must also explore issues of self-identity and what the family means. He must examine his career goals, learn to become psychologically empowered, and cope with health issues. The exercises on the following pages will enhance this process of self-evaluation and development.

LEADERSHIP AND THE AFRICAN AMERICAN MALE

This class will take five two-hour sessions to complete. Its purpose is to develop leadership skills in African American men with an emphasis on family, the community, personal empowerment, and career planning. The goal of this course is to enable African American men to accomplish the following: (1) identify the skills and characteristics of past and present African American male leaders; (2) identify the importance of the African American male's responsibility in maintaining a strong family unit; (3) identify key historical elements of leadership necessary in leading the community, nation, and world; (4) understand the importance of career planning; specifically, develop a vision of the future, learn how to set goals, and build self-esteem; (5) recognize key elements of psychological and spiritual empowerment.

First session: African American Culture, Past and Present. The teacher will lead the men in a discussion of African American culture and highlight the importance of knowing one's history.

Course activities will include the following:

1. The class will discuss African culture and explore the myths of Africa and African people.
2. The class will discuss popular movies (like *Tarzan,* for example) and their implications and stereotypes regarding Africans and Europeans.
3. The class will discuss a list of quotes by African American men (see Appendix One).

Upon completion of this lesson, each student will be required to speak about the importance of his culture and recommend at least one way of reinforcing that importance in the future.

Second session: The African American Contribution. The teacher will introduce the topic of African American contributions to the class. Each student will be given a copy of "Important Dates in African American History" (see Appendix Two). Also, the teacher will involve the students in a study of past and present African American male leaders.

Course activities will include the following:

1. The class will discuss leadership characteristics of past and present African American leaders and view a videotape of selected African American leaders (see Appendix Three).
2. The class will discuss several successful leadership practices.
3. The class will discuss the "Important Dates in African American History" fact sheet.

Upon completion of this lesson, each student will be required to speak to the group about the leadership characteristics that match his own interests and recommend at least one way he will use those characteristics in the future. Also, each student will share with the class an African American contribution which he finds fascinating. A short quiz may be given if the teacher thinks it is necessary (see Appendix Four).

Third session: The African American Man and Family Responsibility. The teacher will introduce the topic of the responsibilities of the African American male. Each student will write a list of key responsibilities that males should have in their families. At the conclusion of the lesson, students will be divided into groups and asked to come up with the most important responsibilities of males in the home. Each group will select a spokesperson who will present its recommendations to the class.

Course activities will include the following:

1. The class will participate in a discussion of the responsibilities of the African American male within the family.
2. Students will be asked to complete a worksheet about the key responsibilities of males in the family (see Appendix Five).
3. Students will be asked to break up into groups to discuss the handout entitled "African American Father's Pledge," "Home Rules for Children," and "Health Maintenance" (see Appendices Six and Seven).
4. A representative from each group will present the group's recommendations to the class.

Upon completion of this lesson, each student will give a brief statement on the importance of male responsibility in the family.

Fourth session: The Importance of African American Male Leadership in the Community, Nation, and World. This lesson will involve a panel of community and religious leaders who will discuss with the students different leadership roles in the African American community and how these roles contribute to improving that community.

Course activities will include the following:

1. The teacher will discuss the importance of African American male leadership in the community, nation, and world.
2. Each panel member will share personal background information and discuss his role in the community and why he chose his particular field.
3. Students will have time to question the panel members about specific areas of interest.
4. Each panel member will share with students his philosophy of the importance of African American male leadership in the community.

Upon completion of this lesson, each student will be asked to state a minimum of two reasons why it is important to have African American male leadership in the community, nation, and world.

Fifth session: Psychological Empowerment. The teacher (or a guest lecturer) will involve the men in a discussion about psychological empowerment with the emphasis on understanding different aspects of power and how people can overcome many obstacles in life. Students will be asked to complete a psychological empowerment inventory worksheet (see Appendix Eight) and present their answers to the class.

Course activities will include the following:

1. The teacher will lead the men in a discussion of psychological empowerment.
2. The men will be asked to break up into groups to discuss the "List of Terms Toward Upward Mobility" (see Appendix Nine). A group representative will share the impact of key words upon members of the group.
3. Each man will complete a psychological empowerment inventory and present it to the class.

Upon completion of this lesson, each man will be asked to describe at least two aspects of psychological empowerment.

SPIRITUALITY

The African American man must be a prime force in his own preservation. He must recognize that to overcome his plight and the difficulties in our society, he will have to make some changes in his lifestyle and spirituality. One important way in which black men can begin to overcome their problems is through Bible study, both private and public.

Public Bible study involves various groups of men coming together in the church for the purpose of sharing God's word. When black men meet together in such fellowship, they demonstrate that they are concerned about their survival and that of their families. Within the context of these meetings, black men can confront such diverse issues as male/female relationships, drugs and violence, imprisonment, male rites of passage, and poverty in the community. They meet outside their roles as deacons, trustees, presidents, and directors and come together in fellowship to discuss issues that are important to black men. In addition to these group meetings, private Bible study is important because it helps the men remember, practice, and be faithful to what they have learned in their group studies.

SPIRITUALITY AND THE AFRICAN AMERICAN MALE

This class will take six one-hour sessions to complete. Its purpose is to explore issues that affect the Christian's life. It is designed to utilize group sharing and silent time for reflection and meditation. The goal of this course is to enable African American men to accomplish the following: (1) interpret present situations on the basis of God's saving acts for a balanced spiritual life; (2) recall their state of oppression throughout history and identify God's grace-filled acts of deliverance on their behalf; (3) explore how African American men can live the Christian life; (4) guide the individual participant in prayerfully considering his own experience in Christ; (5) enable African American men to give an accounting for the hope that is within them; and (6) deepen the participant's life in the Spirit so he can embark upon and further his journey of discipleship.

First session: Sharing Our Journey: The Amazing Grace of God. The teacher will involve the men in a discussion about the uniqueness of their lives and the many ways they are led to God. He will describe the ways in which who they are and from where they have come contribute to the depth of their experiences. The teacher will then guide the group in a discussion of God's grace and what it means to be separated from that grace.

Course activities will include the following:

1. The teacher will present information about grace and how God's acts of deliverance appeared throughout the history of the Israelites.
2. Each man will share the graceful acts of God that he has experienced in his life.
3. Each man will be asked to categorize the acts of grace discussed by the group.

Upon the completion of this session, each student will share what he learned from the lesson on the amazing grace of God.

Second session: How We Understand Faith; Faith and Works in Spiritual Life Development; Aspects of Grace. The teacher will lead the students in a discussion to understand the role that a Christian's faith and good works play in one's everyday life. The teacher will also explain how faith and works can be equalized to produce a balanced life.

Course activities will include the following:

1. The teacher will present biblical concepts of faith and works.
2. Each man will be asked to imagine a teeter-totter with "faith" at one end and "works" at the other. They will consider the roles of faith and works in their own lives and explain which of the two concepts is dominant for them.
3. The men will be asked to break up into groups to discuss how faith and works can be balanced in their lives.

4. A representative from each group will present the group's recommendations to the class.

After reading "We've Come This Far by Faith" (see Appendix Ten), each student will be asked to explain one way in which he expresses faith in his daily living.

Third session: Emotions and Focused Spirituality. The teacher will lead the men in a discussion of the difference between emotion and emotionalism. The men will participate in activities that allow them to integrate what they know about God with what they "feel" about God.

Course activities will include the following:

1. Each student will be asked to read Psalm 1, Mark 1:35-37, and Matthew 6:1-21.
2. After reading these passages, each student will be asked to list the ways in which one's spiritual life is maintained.
3. Each student will be asked to provide at least two ideas about solitude and silence that come to him from the scripture.

Upon the completion of this lesson, each man will present a brief statement concerning what blocks authentic spirituality for him and how he deals with its absence in his life.

Fourth session: Developing a Disciplined Life. The teacher will involve the students in a discussion about the importance of maintaining a disciplined life. The men will participate in activities that allow them to begin their disciplined life through meditation and prayer.

Course activities will include the following:

1. Students will be divided into groups to discuss the ways in which they can maintain a disciplined life.
2. A representative from each group will present the group's recommendations to the class.
3. Those who have made their confession of faith will be asked to participate in a Holy Communion Service or a Service of Dedication (see Appendix Eleven).

Upon the completion of this lesson, each man will be asked to commit a definite time each day (at least fifteen to twenty minutes) for meditation with God. Also, the men will be asked to establish a weekly or monthly meeting time for group fellowship and Bible study to affirm and support each other.

Fifth session: Ministering on the Job. The teacher will lead the men in a discussion about the biblical basis for ministry. The men will participate in activities that explain how God wants them to minister in their jobs. These activities will demonstrate that there is nothing "second class" about being a "lay minister" rather than an ordained member of the clergy.

Course activities will include the following:

1. The class will be asked to answer three questions on a worksheet (see Appendix Twelve). Then they will be paired together to discuss their answers.
2. The whole group will then participate in a discussion of the three questions in an attempt to understand other people's feelings.
3. The class will listen to a fifteen-minute tape entitled "How Two Christians Do It." Then the men will complete the interview exercise in Appendix Twelve and discuss how the two interviews on the tape highlight three principles of vocational ministry.
4. Prior to the end of the session, each man will answer four questions to help discover ways to minister through his daily work (see Appendix Thirteen). Then each man will write down his name and two activities he performs each day at work in the spaces provided on a mini-poster.

Upon completion of this lesson, each man will be asked to commit to ministering through his work for the next twenty-eight days.

Sixth session: Trained to Minister. The teacher will present a mini-lecture on discipleship that will include the biblical concept of "sending" (Jn. 17:18 and 20:21; Acts 11:21-22 and 13:2-3). He will give particular attention to discussing the distinction between calling and sending.

Course activities will include the following:

1. The teacher will play a cassette called "Priorities for Lay Ministers." After listening to the tape, each man will be asked to find a solitary

place in the church where he can reflect on the tape and simply meditate on God's voice.

2. As he considers the Lord's will for his life, each man will attempt to discover what God is telling him to do in his ministry. The men should use this time to reflect on God's leadership in their lives and to affirm his wishes for them.

3. The teacher will distribute a worksheet which suggests four areas of ministry (family, work, other personal relationships and organizations, and church) in which each man might achieve his goals (see Appendix Fourteen).

4. The teacher will lead the class into a spirit of worship introduced with a brief explanation of the meaning of "covenant." This introduction will be followed by a minute of silence in which each person makes his own private covenant with God.

5. The class will participate in a commissioning service in which they will form groups of three or four. Each person will then share his ministry priorities, and the group members will commission each other for ministry, as in Acts 13:2-3. Lastly, each person will pray for the person on his left, and the teacher will close the commissioning service with silent prayer followed by a benediction: "Jesus looks down upon this fellowship this evening and says to us what he said to those first disciples, 'Peace be with you! As the Father has sent me, I am sending you.'"

Upon completion of this lesson, each man will be asked to confirm his covenant with God by filling out a "Ministry Covenant" card (see Appendix Fifteen).

Part Three:

Appendices

Appendix One:

Culture

As African Americans, our understanding of culture is severely limited. Traditionally, black culture as a force for survival and development has been given very little prominence in the education of the young. African American youth have instead long received an education that was a product of the dominant white culture.

The politics and the economics that people experience are the unique results of a society's culture. The language, science, and technology that bring meaning or control to people's lives are also dependent on the culture.

One problem with the concept of culture is that to most of us it is abstract and unobservable. Yet we all experience its manifestations in our clothing, art, music, housing, weapons, films, literature, language, food, politics, educational and social organizations, and economic environment.

To explore the difficulties that African Americans encounter when discussing these concepts of culture, please discuss the following quotes:

Those who do not know history and do not learn from history will repeat it. What is your history?

—George Santayana[1]

If you do not know who you were, it is likely you do not know where you are going. And if you do not know where you are going, any old fool can take you there, and once you arrive you still will be lost, and neither history nor your children will forgive you for being lost.

—Haki R. Madhubuti[2]

A major concern among an oppressed people is that of self-identity: the basic question of "Who am I?" which initiates the definitional process is highly significant.

—Carroll M. Felton, Jr.[3]

History is not the past; history is the present—you and I are history.

—Haki R. Madhubuti[4]

E. Bolaji Idowu, the Nigerian, was shocked into reality as he listened to a film in which Jesus spoke "American" rather than "British" English. He realized that Nigerians need a Christ who speaks redemptively to Nigerians in their cultural setting.

—J. Deotis Roberts[5]

"Culture," "shared understanding," is a medium in which values are transmitted from generation to generation. A people's consciousness, the way they view and operate in the world is shaped by them (or another's) culture.

—Haki R. Madhubuti[6]

The old saying, "The best way to hide something from black people is to put it in a book," is quickly becoming reality.

—Haki R. Madhubuti[7]

A mindless people is a people that joins rather than initiates, obeys rather than questions, follows rather than leads, begs rather that takes.

—Haki R. Madhubuti[8]

Appendix Two:

Important Dates in African American History[9]

1565: Black explorers accompany Spanish explorer Pedro Menéndez de Avilés during the founding of St. Augustine, Florida.

1619: Twenty Africans arrive in Jamestown, Virginia and become the first slaves in North America.

1663: Slaves and white indentured servants plan a rebellion in Gloucester County, Virginia.

1731: Benjamin Banneker, inventor and scientist, is born November 9.

1746: Toussaint L'Ouverture, revolutionary leader of Haiti, is born May 20.

1770: Crispus Attucks is the first to die in the Boston Massacre (during the Revolutionary War).

1773: Chicago is founded by Jean Baptiste Pointe du Sable, a black pioneer from Haiti.

1787: Sojourner Truth, abolitionist and former slave, is born November 18.

1794: The African Methodist Episcopal denomination is founded in Philadelphia by Rev. Richard Allen.

1807: The United States Congress bans importation of slaves. British parliament abolishes the slave trade.

1820: The first United States blacks arrive in Liberia, West Africa. United States Congress enacts the Missouri Compromise, forbidding slavery north of Missouri.

1822: Denmark Vesey's planned slave revolt is uncovered in Charleston, South Carolina. Thirty-seven blacks, including Vesey, are executed.

1827: *Freedom's Journal*, the first black newspaper, is published.

1831: Nat Turner's slave uprising takes place. Fifty-five whites are killed before the rebels are caught. Nat Turner is hanged.

1834: Slavery is abolished throughout the British Empire.

1841: The United States Supreme Court declares freedom for slaves who revolted aboard the ship *Amistad* and orders their return to Africa.

1847: Frederick Douglass publishes the first issue of *North Star*.

1854: Lincoln University, the first black college, is founded as Ashmun Institute in Chester County, Pennsylvania.

1857: The United States Supreme Court rules against Dred Scott (who had been residing in Minnesota, a free territory) and returns him to slavery.

1863: President Abraham Lincoln issues the Emancipation Proclamation.

1865: The United States Congress passes the 13th Amendment, abolishing slavery in the United States.

1870: The 15th Amendment, giving blacks the right to vote, is ratified by the United States Congress.

1873: Slavery is abolished in Puerto Rico.

1883: Jan Matzeliger patents the shoe-lasting machine.

1888: Slavery is abolished in Brazil.

1893: Dr. Daniel Hale Williams performs the first successful open heart surgery.

1909: The NAACP is founded.

1913: Rosa Parks is born February 4. Harriet Tubman, the Underground Railroad "Conductor," dies.

1916: *Journal of Negro History* is first published.

1923: Garrett A. Morgan patents the traffic light.

1926: Dr. Carter G. Woodson begins Negro History Week.

1948: A United States Supreme Court decision gives blacks the right to study law at state institutions.

1950: Gwendolyn Brooks wins the Pulitzer Prize for poetry.

1953: A United States Supreme Court ruling bans segregation in Washington, D.C. restaurants.

1955: Marian Anderson debuts as the first black singer at the Metropolitan Opera House. Rosa Parks is arrested in Montgomery, Alabama for refusing to give her bus seat to a white man.

1957: The United States Congress passes the Civil Rights Act. Nine children integrate Central High School in Little Rock, Arkansas. Ghana, the first British colonial territory, becomes an independent African nation.

1960: Four North Carolina A&T students begin the Sit-in Movement in Greensboro. The Sharpeville Massacre occurs in South Africa. Over sixty people are killed.

1962: Nelson Mandela, the renowned South African freedom fighter, is imprisoned.

1963: Medgar W. Evers, the civil rights leader, is assassinated in Jackson, Mississippi. Four black girls are killed in a Birmingham, Alabama church bombing. Dr. Martin Luther King, Jr. leads a march on Washington, D.C., which becomes the largest civil rights demonstration in history.

1964: Dr. Martin Luther King, Jr. wins the Nobel Peace Prize.

1966:   Edward W. Brooke becomes the first black United States senator since Reconstruction.

1968:   Dr. Martin Luther King, Jr. is assassinated April 4.

1976:   The Soweto uprising in South Africa takes place. Two hundred unarmed schoolchildren are killed.

1983:   Lt. Col. Guion S. Bluford, Jr. becomes the first black astronaut in space.

1986:   Dr. Martin Luther King, Jr.'s birthday (January 15) is celebrated as a legal national holiday in the United States.

1990:   Nelson Mandela is released (February 11) after more than 27 years in prison. He makes his historic visit to the United States in June.

Appendix Three:

Leadership Characteristics of Past and Present African American Male Leaders[10]

1. Loves himself and African American people (the community).

2. Loves his family—wife, children, and relatives.

3. Is spiritually guided and enriched—believes in a supreme being.

4. Is charismatic—inspires others with his message.

5. Believes in the future progress of African American people.

6. Demonstrates good public speaking skills.

7. Believes in hard work—works late hours when necessary.

8. Believes in commitment—does whatever it takes to complete a task or get the job done.

9. Loves young people.

10. Believes that education is vital in making contributions to the improvement of self and the community.

11. Always reaches out to help others in the community who are less fortunate.

12. Often writes books or articles that share his philosophy, his way of life, and his thoughts about important matters.

Appendix Four:

Quiz on Leadership Characteristics of Past and Present African American Male Leaders[11]

Instructions: Please answer the following by identifying each as true (T) or false (F).

1. _____ African American male leaders don't believe in themselves or their community.

2. _____ African American male leaders believe in hard work.

3. _____ African American male leaders are spiritually guided and enriched.

4. _____ African American male leaders don't love young people.

5. _____ African American male leaders have charisma.

6. _____ African American male leaders are not good public speakers.

7. _____ African American male leaders don't like to write articles or books to share their philosophy with others.

8. _____ African American male leaders believe in the future progress of African American people.

9. _____ African American male leaders reach out to help others in the community who are less fortunate.

10. _____ African American male leaders don't believe in commitment.

Appendix Five:

The African American Male, Family Responsibility, and Appropriate Behavior toward Females[12]

Instructions: Please answer the following by identifying each as true (T) or false (F).

1. _____ The African American male's role is outside the home.

2. _____ African American males are smarter than African American females.

3. _____ If an African American boy cries, he is weak.

4. _____ African American males should know how to cook.

5. _____ African American males should fight to settle disagreements.

6. _____ All African American males are leaders.

7. _____ African American fathers are not supposed to rear their children, because this is a mother's responsibility.

8. _____ African American fathers should hug their sons and daughters.

9. _____ African American females should not play sports.

10. _____ An African American father should be the only one who works to earn money for the family.

11. _____ African American males should sell drugs to make money.

12. _____ African American boys should watch television as long as they want each day.

13. _____ African American boys and girls should not do homework.

14. _____ African American boys and girls should respect adults.

15. _____ African American males should love themselves.

Appendix Six:

African American Father's Pledge[13]

I will work to be the best father I can be. Fathering is a daily mission, and there are no substitutes for good fathers. Since I have not been taught to be a father, in order to make my "on the job training" easier, I will study, listen, observe, and learn from my mistakes.

I will openly display love and caring for my wife and children. I will listen to my wife and children. I will hug and kiss my children often. I will be supportive of the mother of my children and spend quality time with my children.

I will teach by example. I will try to introduce myself and my family to something new and developmental each week. I will help my children with their homework and encourage them to be involved in extracurricular activities.

I will read to or with my children as often as possible. I will provide opportunities for my children to develop creatively in the arts: music, dance, drama, literature, and the visual arts. I will challenge my children to do their best.

I will encourage and organize frequent family activities for the home and away from home. I will try to make life a positive adventure and make my children aware of their extended family.

I will never be intoxicated or "high" in the presence of my children, nor will I use language unbecoming for an intelligent and serious father.

I will be non-violent in my relationship with my wife. As a father, my role will be to stimulate and encourage my children rather than carry the "big stick."

I will maintain a home that is culturally in tune with the best African American history, struggle, and future. This will be done, in part, by developing a library of books, records and compact discs, videos, and art collections that reflect the developmental aspects of African American people worldwide. There will be order and predictability in our home.

I will teach my children to be responsible, disciplined, fair, and honest. I will teach them the value of hard work and fruitful production. I will teach them the importance of family, community, politics, economics, and religion. I will teach them the importance of the Nguzo Saba (black value system) and the role that ownership of property and business plays in our struggle.

As a father, I will attempt to provide my family with an atmosphere of love and security to aid them in their development into sane, loving, productive, spiritual, hard-working, creative African Americans who realize they have a responsibility to do well and help the less fortunate of this world. I will teach my children to be activists and to think for themselves.

Appendix Seven:

Health Maintenance[14]

1. Get six to eight hours of sleep a night.

2. Drink at least a half gallon of clean water a day. Remember, most tap water is polluted.

3. Bathe every day—seek cleanliness.

4. Exercise at least forty-five minutes, four times a week.

5. Start each day with fifteen minutes of deep breathing; try to bring life-giving oxygen into your system.

6. Avoid, if possible, most processed foods. Move toward a diet of fifty percent cooked food, fifty percent uncooked food. Start each day with fruit and fresh juices. Always under-eat rather than stuff yourself.

7. Be creative—creativity and longevity go hand in hand.

8. Study—always seek life-giving and life-saving information. Be disciplined.

Diseases which are commonly prevented, consistently impeded, and sometimes cured by a low-fat vegetarian diet include the following:

Strokes	Constipation
Kidney stones	Diverticulosis
Prostate cancer	Hypertension
Cervical cancer	Salmonellosis
Diabetes	Osteoporosis
Peptic ulcers	Colon cancer
Hiatal hernias	Ovarian cancer
Gallstones	Endometrial cancer
Irritable colon syndrome	Kidney disease
Heart disease	Hemorrhoids
Breast cancer	Obesity
Pancreatic cancer	Asthma
Stomach cancer	Trichinosis
Hypoglycemia	

Appendix Eight:

Psychological Empowerment[15]

The following exercises will enable you to conduct a psychological profile of yourself and help you to identify your motivation.

PERSONAL ANALYSIS

1. How do I view myself?

2. What are my strengths?

3. How did I come by my strengths?

4. Am I focused on survival or mastery?

5. Have I dealt with the demons that are associated with being aggressive?

6. How do I move beyond being the victim?

INTERPERSONAL ANALYSIS

1. How do people relate to me?

2. How do I relate to other people?

3. How well do I listen?

4. When and where do I feel tension in my relationships?

KEY POINTS

- Mastery is much more proactive than survival—it relates to your ability to view things from the top down.

- Getting in touch with yourself is an asset rather than a liability.

- There is a great need to understand aggression psychologically.

- Develop the ability to out-think people.

- Develop a peer group with whom you can share personal and inter-personal experiences.

- Continue to monitor your aspirations.

Appendix Nine:

Dr. Johnson's Vocabulary List of Terms toward Upward Mobility[16]

Achieve	Do, accomplish, succeed
Action	Doing
Actualize	To fulfill
Adaptability	Ability to adjust or fit in
Adamant	Inflexible
Ambitious	Having a desire to achieve a particular goal
Apply	Put to use
Arête	Supreme excellence
Aspiration	A strong desire to achieve something high or great
Attendance	The act of being present, frequency
Attitude	Mental posture, way of thinking
Awareness	Mindfulness, consciousness, level of realization
Astute	Keenly aware, having clear and precise vision
Behavior	Ways, actions, mannerisms
Bona fide	Unfaked, sure-enough, pure
Business-like	Orderly, well-regulated
Career	Course, job flow, education flow

Communication	Two-way exchange of information and ideas
Competitive	Inclined, desiring, or suited to complete
Conceive	To imagine
Conduct	Pattern of behavior
Constructive	Promoting improvement or development
Conscientious	Exact, accurate, precise, correct
Consistency	Persistence, steadiness
Continuity	Persistence without change, uninterrupted duration of time
Coordination	To bring into a common action, movement, or condition
Creativity	Having the quality of something created rather than initiated
Charisma	A magnetic charm or appeal, a personal magic of leadership
Decorum	Rules of conduct
Determination	The act of making or arriving at a decision
Diligent	Characterized by being earnest and energetic
Direction	Forward, outlook
Discipline	Self-control, self-mastery
Durable	Long-lasting
Earnest	The act of deserving, serious intent
Employment	The work in which one is engaged
Empowerment	The move forward with one's power
Endurance	The ability to withstand hardship or stress
Experience	The act of knowing how
Exposure	The act of discovering differences
First class	Top-notch
Flexibility	The ability to change with notice
Follow-up	To carry to completion
Function	Action intended to be performed
Goal	The end toward which an effort is directed
Humane	Having consideration for other human beings

Initiative	The act of facilitating the beginning
Integrity	Soundness, firm adherence to moral values
Intellect	One's capacity for knowledge
Labor	Human activity that provides the goods or services in an economy; workers employed in an establishment
Logic	The act of rationalizing, using common sense
Mastery	The victorious use of one's skills
Mission	A specific task to which a person is devoted
Motivation	The incentive or drive to do something
Management	A judicious use of means to accomplish
Negotiations	To arrange for, buy, or bring about through conference, discussion, or compromise
Nerve	Power or endurance and control
Opportunity	A chance for advancement or progress
Optimum	Maximum, best
Participation	The act of taking part or being part of a larger whole
Patience	Steadfast despite opposition, difficulty, or adversity; the capacity to sustain
Performance	The execution of actions
Perfection	The act of exemplifying supreme excellence
Perseverance	To persist or endure in an undertaking in spite of counter influences, opposition, or discouragement
Personality	The totality of an individual's behavioral and emotional tendencies
Positive	The act of expressing one's existence or quality
Potential	Something that can develop or become actual through pursuit
Pride	Reasonable and justifiable self-esteem
Planning	The act or process of making or carrying out planned actions

Priority	Preferential ranking over another
Preparation	The act of being ready, readiness
Proactive	To take the initiative
Productivity	The state of performing work or efforts
Prosperity	The condition of being successful or thriving; economic well-being
Punctuality	Being on time, prompt
Quality	Superiority in kind
Quantity	Determinate or estimated amount
Quest	To search for an end result
Reference	Framework or source of information
Regulations	An authoritative rule dealing with details or procedures, rules of order
Reliable	Giving the same result on successive trials
Renaissance	Rebirth; a movement of new and revised interests
Respect	To consider something worthy of high regard; expressions of consideration of others
Responsibility	Reliability, trustworthiness, accountability
Reputation	Overall quality or character as seen or judged by people; in general, developing a good name
Rules	A prescribed guide for conduct or action
Retention	Holding power—as of a job or knowledge
Self-actualize	To recognize fully one's potential
Self-concept	The mental image one has of oneself
Skill	The ability to execute learned physical tasks
Sophisticated	Worldly wise, finely experienced and aware, unfoolable
Success	The attainment of goals—work, education, wealth, family
Supervision	The process of directing a course of action
Tangible	Capable of being precisely realized by the mind

Time	A person's experience during a specified period, duration of efforts
Tolerance	Capacity to endure hardship or pain, stamina to complete tasks such as work, education, or goals
Upward mobility	The art of moving or thinking toward the highest point of realization; to be greater
Value	To rate or scale in importance, or general worth, to consider or rate highly
Versatility	Turning with ease from one thing to another
Vision	The ability to see one's future in front of one
Work	The activity in which one exerts strength or faculties to do or perform something
Workmanship	The quality imparted to a thing in the process of working
Zeal	The passion of eagerness and interest in pursuit of something
Zenith	The highest point that can be reached

Appendix Ten:

We've Come this Far by Faith[17]

A church historian, defining the difference between tradition and traditionalism, said that tradition is the living faith of the dead while traditionalism is the dead faith of the living. Faith is alive in the first; it is dead in the second. I would argue that the distinction between the two is pertinent to our churches today.

The old spirituals, the evolution of the black church, and the rich oral tradition out of which our preaching comes are but a few of the treasures of our spiritual heritage. The old spirituals were born out of a solid foundation of childlike and profound faith. Our fathers and mothers, whose lives were forged on the anvil of suffering, felt God at deep levels. They found spiritual sustenance in even the most difficult times, and they experienced God at an intensely personal level.

One of the great problems of today is that many who occupy pews on Sunday morning have not experienced God deep within their souls. They are nominal Christians who, through their lack of deep and abiding faith, manifest the dead faith of the living.

The Israelites, who were the children of God, were delivered safely from Egypt. God sustained them in their wilderness wanderings, fulfilling their physical and spiritual needs. Today, God delivers us as he did the Israelites. The hymns and spirituals to which we listen, like "Oh, Mary, Don't You Weep, Don't You Mourn," remind us of this spiritual heritage of deliverance. Our lives today need to be built upon the foundation of God's word and on Christ, the author and finisher of faith.

Our culture glorifies the spirit of "do-it-yourself-ism." Many church members base their salvation on their own efforts, believing that their faith is something which comes from within. They don't realize that biblical faith comes from God. Faith is God-centered optimism, as our spirituals and gospel songs tell us.

Faith is what leads us to God, and its goal is the realization of God's kingdom. Faith allows that kingdom to exist within you and me; therefore, through faith, God gives meaning and direction to our lives.

The vitality of faith, fueled by its optimistic outlook, encourages us to make the kingdom of God a reality in our world. Faith is not static or passive; it is dynamic, working toward future goals. This understanding of faith was a key concept for Mordecai W. Johnson. Faith for blacks, in Johnson's thinking, is tied to our historical faith in the God of holiness and justice. This faith demands that we work for the principles of freedom and democracy, that we work for a society based on justice and liberation.

Although our society is currently organized to make the achievement of justice, love, and brotherhood and sisterhood most difficult for minorities to attain, our faith declares that God, who is at the center of the universe, is greater than that society. Despite the abuses (or perhaps because of them) of political, social, economic, and educational power, God still calls us to work for wholeness and healing in the world. It is imperative that God's people work toward freedom and justice as an outgrowth of their faith.

Throughout our history, the leaders in the struggle for freedom and justice for all of God's children were motivated by their unshakable faith in God. They believed that God sees the affliction of his people, hears their cries, and comes to deliver them.

We live in a culture in which people emphasize *belief* rather than *faith*. In some religious circles, one is expected to believe a set of rules—no questions asked. You just need to believe! The problem with this narrow view is that it lacks the experience of God deep within. It is too full of creeds, and it will leave the inner person starved. One cannot relate to what or whom one has never experienced.

It was faith that sustained Dr. Martin Luther King, Jr. and the many blacks and whites who endured emotional, spiritual, and physical trauma in changing and challenging the social climate of this land. Dr. King declared that it was the black church rather than secular forces that brought non-violent protest into being. He reminded the nation that love and justice were the greatest contributions of our Judeo-Christian heritage.

Your actions are a good indicator of what you believe. Faith and action go hand in hand:

> What good is it, my brothers and sisters, if you say you have faith but do not have works? So faith by itself, if it has no works, is dead. (James 2:14, 17)

Observing the difference between what many churches professed and what they actually practiced in the arena of economic and racial justice in our nation, Dr. King wrote the following in a letter from a Birmingham jail:

> I have watched so many churches commit themselves to a completely otherworldly religion which made a strange distinction between body and soul, the sacred and the secular...a religious community largely adjusted to the status quo...rather than...leading men to higher levels of justice.

Men and women who are being faithful to God and to the spirit demonstrate their commitment through their actions in the world around them. Without that action, our faith becomes anemic, and we fall short of our calling as Christians.

Appendix Eleven:

Holy Communion Service

GREETING

Leader:	The grace of the Lord Jesus Christ be with you.
Men:	And also with you.
Leader:	The risen Christ is with us.
Men:	Praise the Lord!

OPENING PRAYER

All: Almighty God, to you all hearts are open, all desires are known, and from you no secrets are hidden. Cleanse the thoughts of our hearts by the inspiration of your Holy Spirit, that we may perfectly love you, and worthily magnify your holy name, through Christ our Lord, amen.

HYMN: "Amazing Grace"

SCRIPTURE READINGS

Old Testament: Isaiah 53
New Testament: Hebrews 10

PRAYERS OF THE MEN

PRAYER OF CONFESSION

Leader: In silence let us make our confession to God.

WORDS OF PARDON

THE PEACE

Leader: Christ our Lord invites to his table all who love him and who desire to live in peace with one another. Therefore, let us offer one another signs of reconciliation and love.

HYMN OR SPECIAL MUSIC: "Take My Life, and Let It Be"

THE GREAT THANKSGIVING

Leader: The Lord be with you.
Men: And also with you.
Leader: Lift up your hearts.
Men: We lift them up to the Lord.
Leader: Let us give thanks to the Lord our God. Therefore, with your people on earth and all the company of heaven, we praise your name and join their unending hymn:
         Holy, holy, holy Lord, God of power and might.
         Heaven and earth are full of your glory.

Hosanna in the highest.
Blessed is he who comes in the name of the Lord.
Hosanna in the highest.

THE LORD'S PRAYER

Our Father in heaven,
hallowed be your name.
Your kingdom come,
your will be done,
on earth as it is in heaven.
Give us today our daily bread.
Forgive us our sins
as we forgive those who sin against us.
Save us from the time of trial
and deliver us from evil.
For the kingdom, the power, and the glory are
yours now and for ever.

BREAKING THE BREAD

GIVING THE BREAD AND CUP

HYMN

BENEDICTION

Appendix Twelve:

Ministering on the Job [18]

I. SECOND-CLASS CHRISTIANS?

Read each of the following statements, then mark whether you feel that way often, sometimes, or never. Your answer should express how you feel, not how you believe intellectually, which may be different.

1. I feel that as a layperson I am sort of a second-class Christian, not quite as important as my pastor.

   I feel this way...
   a. Often
   b. Sometimes
   c. Never

2. My job (or family or school-work) doesn't leave me as much time to minister as I would like to have.

   a. Often
   b. Sometimes
   c. Never

3. I'm only a _____.
   (housewife, student, factory
   worker, businessman, etc.) I can't
   do very much for God.

   a. Often
   b. Sometimes
   c. Never

II. HOW TWO CHRISTIANS DO IT

As you listen to the two interviews, jot down any ideas you might be able to use to minister in your daily activities at work, school, or home.

Interview #1	Interview #2

Appendix Thirteen:

Designing my own Strategy[19]

I. DESIGNING MY OWN STRATEGY: The four questions below will stimulate you to discover for yourself specific ways you can minister more effectively in your daily "work."

1. In what ways can God use the services I perform or the products I produce to meet the needs of others?	3. What are some ways Jesus can touch through me those I contact in my work?
2. If for the next 28 days I make service—meeting the needs of others—my number one goal in my work (above making money, achieving success, etc.), what changes might that bring in the way I approach my job?	4. Are there any other ways I can bring glory to God, or cause others to praise God or think more highly of him, through my work?

II. MY TWENTY-EIGHT DAY PLAN: Fill out the mini poster, then set it or post it where you will see it each day as you work—on a wall, your desk, notebook, lunchpail, etc.

"_____, whether you

(my name)

_____ or _____

(something I do each day at work)   (something I do each day at work)

or whatever you do, do it
all to the glory of God."

For the next 28 days, I will try to glorify God through my work in these ways:

1. _____   3. _____

2. _____   4. _____

Appendix Fourteen:

Sent into Ministry[20]

Please answer the following questions:

I. THE SEND-OFF
    What does it mean to be sent into ministry?

II. MY MINISTRY PRIORITIES
    I believe God has called me to minister to the following…

    To my family by…

Through my work by...

Through other personal relationships and organizations by...

Through my church by...

Appendix Fifteen:

Ministry Covenant[21]

You have identified your call. Are you ready to answer it? Take a moment to confirm a covenant just between you and God. From among those ministries to which God is calling you, include in your covenant only those to which you are ready to commit yourself, either for service or for training.

MINISTRY COVENANT

God, this day I covenant with you to fulfill by your power and to the best of my ability your call to me to minister in the following ways:

_____

_____

_____

_____

Part Four:

Further Guides

Chapter Six:

A Retreat for Men

The following guide can be used in leading an overnight discipleship retreat for African American men. The retreat should take place at a center where meals and adequate sleeping arrangements are furnished. You may also consider utilizing a local Y.M.C.A. Keep in mind, however, that not all Y.M.C.A.s have sleeping facilities, and the participants may have to bring their sleeping bags. Twenty to thirty men can be easily accommodated in this retreat.

INTRODUCTION

The future of the black man is one of the great challenges facing America in this decade and beyond. The persistence of racism, unemployment, school failure, drugs, violence, imprisonment, and low church involvement are a few of the problems that our men must face. If these problems are not addressed and properly dealt with, we are sure to become an endangered species.

Like the Israelites in Egypt before God's deliverance, The African American male has been in bondage. This leadership retreat seeks to focus on the black man's role historically and biblically, which will in turn allow you to understand the black man's place in the present and the future. To gain this understanding, you must be an interpreter of the times—politically, socially, economically, religiously, and racially.

This discipleship retreat will enable you to deepen your inner life and deal with your external circumstances—to "always be ready to make your defense to anyone who demands from you an accounting for the hope that is in you" (I Peter 3:15). It will enable you, like the Israelites, to interpret your present reality on the basis of God's saving acts.

This retreat has been planned to help guide you to prayerfully consider your own experience in Christ. It is designed to utilize group sharing, silent time for reflection, and meditation. Your experience in this retreat will be enhanced by your full participation in the activities, in both group and individual study. The central goals of this retreat are that you will (1) learn something about yourself, (2) understand your place in history, and (3) either "enter" or "further" your commitment to Christian discipleship.

As you embark upon this retreat experience, you are invited to open your mind, heart, and soul to a variety of issues. You are welcome to speak freely!

SUGGESTED RETREAT SCHEDULE [1]

Theme: "Black Men Leading in the '90s"
Name: African American Empowerment Network (A.M.E.N.)

DAY ONE: FRIDAY NIGHT

7:00 P.M.	Participants arrive and complete registration
7:30 P.M.	Dinner, welcome, and introduction of program
8:30 P.M.	First group session: the problems of the black man
9:30 P.M.	Break
9:40 P.M.	Recreation period: basketball, volleyball, swimming, billiards, ping-pong, weight room

11:00 P.M.	Second group session: solutions proposed
Midnight	Individual study, reflection, solitude, and rest

DAY TWO: SATURDAY MORNING

6:30 A.M.	Wake-up call
7:00 A.M.	Individual study and reflection
8:00 A.M.	Breakfast
9:00 A.M.	Third group session: The black man and discipleship
10:00 A.M.	Break
10:30 A.M.	Group reflection and sharing (small groups)
Noon	Lunch
1:00 P.M.	Fourth group session: developing a disciplined life
2:00 P.M.	Break
2:10 P.M.	Closing worship
3:00 P.M.	Homeward bound

Chapter Seven:

Planning a Year's Program

Suggested Ideas

January: Announcement of concern for absence of black men
A King's Holiday Celebration
Questionnaire

February: Celebrate Black History Month
    •Skits during Sunday services
    •Costume "party" with black heroes and heroines
Workshops on self-development
Valentine's Day—the men set up dates with their wives
    and girlfriends[1]

March: Workshops on sociological development
Plan for contemporary Sunday School (echoes Sunday
    School materials)[2]

          Workers' conference and leadership training
Four outings[3]
- Visit to jail
- Visit to hospital
- Visit to youth camp
- Visit to homeless shelter or drug shelter

April: Workshops on spirituality
Easter celebrations
The men set up dates with their wives and girlfriends
Implement contemporary Sunday School
Plan graduate recognition day
All men service

May: Family Day
- Special Sunday service
- Sunday picnic

Graduate Recognition Day
Begin home Bible study[4]
African Liberation Day

June: Father's Day (to be celebrated at the same magnitude of mother's day)
Juneteenth National Freedom Day

July: Men's involvement in Vacation Bible School
Prayer Partner Sunday
Men's retreat

November: Umoja Karamu
Thanksgiving

December: Christmas
Kwanzaa Celebration

Chapter Eight:

Suggested Questionnaire

Please circle the letter that best describes your answer.

1. Are you presently attending a church?

   a. Yes   b. No

2. Did you grow up in church?

   a. Yes   b. No

3. If you attend church, on an average, how often do you attend worship services?

   a. Every week   d. About every six weeks
   b. About twice a month   e. Two to four times a year
   c. About once a month   f. Once a year

4. If you attend church, how long have you attended church on a regular basis?

  a. Less than one year d. Six to nine years
  b. One to three years e. Ten to twenty years
  c. Four to five years f. Twenty-one years or more

5. If you attend church, who influenced you to attend church?

  a. Grandparents c. Parents
  b. Family and friends d. Other _____

6. If you attended church but later left the church, who or what caused you to leave?

  a. Lack of motivation c. Preacher
  b. Program d. Other _____

7. If you later returned to church, why did you return?

  a. Needed Christ/ c. Liked the church
   something missing d. Other _____
   in my life
  b. Spiritual gains

8. The man's role in the church should be:

  a. Role model c. Help church and others
  b. Leadership d. Other _____

9. The purpose(s) that the church serves is(are):

a. Worship and
community service

b. Create other lifestyle

c. Family guidance

d. Other _____

Please complete the following sentences in your own words.

10. I think more black men would attend church if _____

_____

_____

11. I think that black men are absent from the church because

_____

_____

_____

12. I am motivated to be active in church because _____

_____

_____

13. What is your age?

a. 18 - 24
b. 25 - 34
c. 35 - 44

d. 45 - 54
e. 55 -64
f. 65 or older

14. What is your marital status?

a. Single
b. Separated or divorced

c. Widowed
d. Married

15. What is your income before taxes? (Estimate as best you can)

a. Under $7,499   d. $25,000 - $34,999
b. $7,500 - $14,999   e. $35,000 - $49,999
c. $15,000 - $24,999   f. $50,000 or more

16. What is your highest level of formal education?

a. Less than high school   e. Some college
b. Some high school   f. College degree
c. High school graduate   g. Post graduate
d. Trade or vocational   h. Graduate degree
   school

17. Which one of the following best describes you?

a. Retired   c. Employed full-time
b. Employed part-time   d. Unemployed

18. If you are employed, what is your occupation?

_____

Notes

INTRODUCTION

1. Matt. 22:23-30 KJV.
2. Janice Hale-Benson, "The Transmission of Faith to Young Black Children" (paper presented at the Conference on Faith Development in Early Childhood, Henderson, N.C., 1987), 4.
3. Clifford E. McLain, *Until the Men Sit Down* (Kansas City: Jordan Communication Company, 1988), 18.
4. I John 1:6-7 KJV.
5. Heb. 10:24-25 KJV.
6. McLain, 18.
7. Ibid., 18, 25.
8. C. Eric Lincoln and Lawrence H. Mamiya, *The Black Church in the African American Experience* (London: Duke University Press, 1990), 305.

PART ONE, CHAPTER ONE:
BIBLICAL AND THEOLOGICAL MANDATES

1. Luke 6:46-49 TEV (*Today's English Version*).
2. Allen Coppedge, *Biblical Principles of Discipleship* (Grand Rapids: Zondervan, 1989), 19.
3. John Hendrix and Lloyd Householder, *The Equipping of Disciples* (Nashville: Broadman Press, 1977), 16.
4. William L. Banks, *In Search of the Great Commission* (Chicago: Moody Press, 1991), 76-77.
5. Matt. 10:1 and John 1:39 KJV.
6. Matt. 4:19 NEB.
7. Ibid., 8:22.
8. Matt. 9:6 TEV.
9. Ibid., 10:7.
10. Ibid., 11:28.
11. Ibid., 10:7.
12. Ibid., 19:14.
13. Hendrix and Householder, Foreword.
14. Jurgen Moltmann, *Hope for the Church: Moltmann in Dialogue with Practical Theology*, ed. and trans. Theodore Runyon (Nashville: Abingdon, 1979), 132.
15. Matt. 4:17 KJV.
16. Mark 1:14-20 KJV.
17. Matt. 5:3-12, 20-21; 4:23 KJV.
18. T. M. Moore, "Education for Christian Discipleship: A Concept and Tool," *Christian Education Journal* (November 1989): 73.
19. Hendrix and Householder, 82.
20. Matt. 18:20 RSV.
21. Mark 6:7 KJV.
22. Matt. 3:16-19 KJV.
23. Hendrix and Householder, 78.
24. C. Daniel Watson, J. Christian Baker, and W. Malcolm Clark, *Commitment with Ideology* (Philadelphia: Pilgrim Press, 1973), 49.

25. Coppedge, 76.
26. Ibid., 76, 61.
27. Ibid., 61.
28. Ibid., 75.
29. Ibid., 76.
30. Hendrix and Householder, 70.
31. Douglas Milne, "Mark: The Gospel of Servant Discipleship," *The Reformed Theological Review* (January-April 1990): 20.
32. Paul R. Hinlicky, "Conformity to Christ in the Gospel of Mark," *Currents in Theology and Mission* (August 1988): 365.
33. Col. 1:28-29 TEV.
34. Dietrich Bonhoeffer, *Christ the Center* (New York: Harper and Row, 1966), 61.
35. C. Eric Lincoln, *This Road Since Freedom* (Durham, N.C.: Carolina Wren Press, 1990), 38.
36. Gal. 2:20 KJV.
37. Dietrich Bonhoeffer, *The Cost of Discipleship* (New York: MacMillan, 1966), 337.
38. I Cor. 5:17 TEV.
39. II Cor. 3:18 TEV.
40. Dallas Willard, *Spirit of Discipling* (New York: Harper Collins, 1988), 1.
41. Coppedge, 30-36.
42. Willard, 15.

CHAPTER TWO: THE PROBLEM OF DISCIPLING BLACK MEN

1. J. Deotis Roberts, *Black Theology in Dialogue* (Philadelphia: The Westminister Press, 1987), 108.
2. C. Eric Lincoln, *The Black Experience in Religion* (Garden City, N.Y.: Anchor Press/Doubleday, 1971), 1.
3. Robert Staples, *Black Masculinity: The Black Male's Role in American Society* (San Francisco: The Black Scholar Press, 1982), 42.

4. C. Eric Lincoln, *The Black Church Since Frazier* (New York: Schoken Books, 1974), 153.

5. C. Eric Lincoln and Lawrence H. Mamiya, *The Black Church in the African Experience* (London: Duke University Press, 1990), 305.

6. Clifford Eugene McLain, *Until the Men Sit Down* (Kansas City: Jordan Communication Company, 1988), 40.

7. Anthony T. Evans, *America's Only Hope* (Chicago: Moody Press, 1990), 17.

8. Francis Cress Welsing, *The Isis Papers: The Keys to the Colors* (Chicago: Third World Press, 1991), 257.

9. Avery Brooks, *Young Black Men—A Lost Generation* (Cleveland, Ohio: Cleveland Radio Station WHK, November 1990), audiocassette.

10. Haki R. Madhubuti, *Black Men: Obsolete, Single, Dangerous?* (Chicago: Third World Press, 1990), iv.

11. Henry C. Gregory III, "Incarceration and Rehabilitation: A Challenge to the African American Church and Community," in *Black Men in Prison: The Response of the African American Church,* ed. Gayraud Wilmore (Atlanta: The ITC Press, 1990), 13-14.

12. Madhubuti, iv.

13. Jeffrey M. Johnson, *The Black Male: The New Bald Eagle* (Washington, D.C.: Management Plus, 1989), 6.

14. National Urban League, *The State of Black America* (The National Urban League, 1990), 6.

15. Staples, 50.

16. Ibid., 52.

17. Madhubuti, 50.

18. Lincoln and Mamiya, 304.

19. McLain, 27.

20. Ibid., 70.

21. Matt. 28:19-20 KJV.

22. Acts 1:8 KJV.

23. McLain, 58-60.

24. Edward P. Wimberly, *African American Pastoral Care* (Nashville: Abingdon Press, 1991), 60.
25. Jeffrey M. Johnson, 23.
26. Gwendolyn Rice, "Young Black Men, the Church, and Our Future," *Chicago Theological Register* (Spring 1988): 12.

CHAPTER THREE: CONTEMPORARY MODELS

1. Francis Cress Welsing, *The Isis Papers: The Keys to the Colors* (Chicago: Third World Press, 1991), 284.
2. Carroll M. Felton, Jr., *The Care of Souls in the Black Church* (New York: Martin Luther King Press, 1980), 11.
3. Ibid., 294.
4. J. Deotis Roberts, *Roots of a Black Future: Family and Church* (Philadelphia: The Westminister Press, 1980), 85.
5. Haki R. Madhubuti, *Exploring the Negative Impact of the Black Men's Guide to Understanding the Black Woman* (Chicago: Third World Press, 1990), 19.
6. James Cone, *Black Theology: A Documentary History 1960-1979* (Maryknoll, N.Y.: Orbis Books, 1979), 94.
7. Roberts, 94.
8. II Cor. 5:19 KJV.
9. David Watson, *Called & Committed: World Changing Discipleship* (Wheaton: Harold Shaw Publishers, 1982), 58.
10. John Hendrix and Lloyd Householder, *The Equipping of Disciples* (Nashville: Broadman Press, 1977), 40.
11. Robert Staples, *Black Masculinity* (San Francisco: The Black Scholar Press, 1982), 78.
12. Haki R. Madhubuti, *Black Men: Obsolete, Single, Dangerous?* (Chicago: Third World Press, 1990), 167.
13. Jeremiah Wright, interview by author, 19 October 1991.
14. Ibid.
15. E. K. Bailey, interview by author, 3 January 1992.
16. Ibid.

17. Ibid.
18. Ibid.
19. Ibid.
20. Kelly Brown, interview by author, 19 July 1991.
21. Ibid.
22. Ibid.
23. Ibid.
24. Ibid.

PART TWO, CHAPTER FOUR: HOW TO BEGIN

1. Prov. 29:18 KJV.
2. E. K. Bailey, interview by author, 8 January 1992.
3. II Cor. 5:19 KJV.
4. John 1:40-41 KJV.

PART THREE: APPENDICES

1. Carroll M. Felton, Jr., *The Care of Souls in the Black Church* (New York: Martin Luther King Press, 1980), 284.
2. Haki R. Madhubuti, *Exploring the Negative Impact of the Black Man's Guide to Understanding the Black Woman* (Chicago: Third World Press, 1990), 18.
3. Felton, 11.
4. Madhubuti, 19.
5. Deotis J. Roberts, *Roots of a Black Future: Family and Church* (Philadelphia: The Westminister Press), 94.
6. Madhubuti, 19.
7. Ibid., 50.
8. Haki R. Madhubuti, *Black Men: Obsolete, Single, Dangerous?* (Chicago: Third World Press, 1990), 167.
9. Hudson, Wade, and Cheryl Willis Hudson, eds., *Black History Activity and Enrichment Handbook* (New Jersey: Just Us Books, Inc., 1990), 40-41.

10. Jeffrey M. Johnson, *The Black Male: The New Bald Eagle* (Washington: Management Plus, 1989), 81.
11. Ibid., 82.
12. Ibid., 83.
13. Madhubuti, *Black Men*, 193.
14. Ibid., 204.
15. Johnson, 85-86.
16. Ibid., 89-91.
17. Robert E. Dungy, *Dimensions of Spirituality in the Black Experience, Leader's Guide* (Nashville: Upper Room Books, 1991), 31-34.
18. James L. Garlow, *Partners in Ministry: Laity & Pastors Working Together* (Kansas City: Beacon Hill Press, 1981), Appendix B, student resource sheet no. 2. Used by permission of the publisher.
19. Ibid., student resource sheet no. 2B.
20. Ibid., student resource sheet nos. 2, 2B.
21. Ibid., student resource sheet no. 7B.

Part Four, Chapter Six: A Retreat for Men

1. The time frame for this schedule is established by the men during their monthly meetings.

Chapter Seven: Planning a Year's Program

1. Men must begin dating their wives or girlfriends weekly.
2. As an alternative to traditional Sunday School, contemporary issues will be discussed (including divorce, unmarried status, money management, stress, etc.).
3. Each weekend, an outing will be taken to one of each of the following: a jail, a hospital, a youth camp, and a homeless shelter or drug rehabilitation clinic. Note that the hospital visit should take place in an emergency room at midnight on a Saturday night.
4. Families will be given family candles to light each Saturday evening as a symbol of the church in study.

Bibliography

Anderson, Ray S. *Theological Foundation for Ministry*. Grand Rapids, MI: Erdman's Publishing Co., 1979.

Bailey, E. K. *The Challenge and Art of Discipling Black Men*. Dallas: Concord Missionary Baptist Church, 1982.

Banks, William L. *In Search of the Great Commission*. Chicago: Moody Press, 1991.

Bonhoeffer, Dietrich. *The Cost of Discipleship*. New York: MacMillan Publishing Co., Inc., 1961.

Burrow, Rufus. "Sexism in the Black Community and the Black Church." *Interdenominational Theological Seminars Journal* 13 (1986): 317-322.

Christenson, Evelyn. *Lord, Change Me!* Wheaton, IL: Victor, 1979.

Collyn, Kruse. *New Testament Models for Ministry*. Nashville: Thomas Nelson Publishers, 1983.

Cone, James. *Black Theology: A Documentary History 1960-1979*. Maryknoll, NY: Orbis Books, 1979.

Coppedge, Allan. *Biblical Principles of Discipleship*. Grand Rapids, MI: Zondervan, 1989.

Davies, Richard E. *Handbook for Doctor of Ministry Project: An Approach to Structured Observation of Ministry*. Latham, MO: University Press of America, 1984.

Dulles, Avery. *Models of the Church*. Garden City, NY: Doubleday & Company, 1974.

————. "Community of Disciples as a Model of Church." Journal of *Philosophy and Theology* 14 (1986): 99-120.

Dungy, Robert E. *Dimensions of Spirituality in the Black Experience*. Nashville: Upper Room Books, 1991.

Dunston, Alfred G., Jr. *The Black Man in the Old Testament and Its World*. Philadelphia: Dorrance and Company, 1974.

Eight Translation New Testament: King James Version, The Living Bible, Phillips Standard Version, Revised Standard Version, Today's English Version, New International Version, Jerusalem Bible, New English Bible. Wheaton, IL: Tyndale House Publishers, Inc., 1974.

Evans, Anthony T. *America's Only Hope*. Chicago: Moody Press, 1990.

Felton, Carroll M., Jr. *The Care of Souls in the Black Church*. New York: Martin Luther King Press, 1980.

Forest, Martin. "Learning From the Struggle in Bonhoeffer's Christological Ethic." *Journal of Theology for Southern Africa* 58 (1987): 57-72.

Franklin, Robert Michael, Jr. *Why Men Leave the Church: A Diagnostic Study*. Chicago: University of Chicago, 1981.

Frazier, Franklin E. *The Negro Church in America*. New York: Schocken Books, 1972.

Garlow, James L. *Partners in Ministry: Laity and Pastors Working Together*. Kansas City: Beacon Hill Press, 1981.

Gary, Lawrence E. *Black Men*. Beverly Hills: Sage Publishing, Inc., 1986.

Gibbs, Jewelle Taylor. *Young, Black and Male in America: An Endangered Species*. New York: Auburn House, 1988.

Gregory, Henry C. III. "Incarceration and Rehabilitation: A Challenge to the African American Church and Community." In *Black*

Men in Prison: The Response of the African American Church, edited by Gayraud Wilmore. Atlanta: The ITC Press, 1990.

Hale-Benson, Janice. "The Transmission of Faith to Young Black Children." Paper presented at the Conference on Faith Development in Early Childhood, Vance-Grandville College, Henderson, North Carolina, December 1987.

Haney, David. *The Lord and His Laity*. Nashville: Broadman Press, 1978.

Hendrix, John, and Lloyd Householder. *The Equipping of Disciples*. Nashville: Broadman Press, 1977.

Hepburn, Bob. "Penetrating an Urban People Group: The Street-Oriented, Young Black Male." *Urban Mission* 23 (1989): 33-42.

Hinlicky, Paul R. "Conformity to Christ in the Gospel of Mark." *Currents in Theology and Mission* 15 (1988): 364-368.

Johnson, Jeffrey M. *The Black Male: The New Bald Eagle*. Washington: Management Plus, 1989.

Johnson, John H. "An African American Father's Pledge." *Ebony Man Magazine* 7 (1992): 50.

Jones, Major. *Black Awareness: A Theology of Hope*. Nashville: Abingdon Press, 1971.

Kvalbein, Hans. "Go Therefore and Make Disciples: The Concept of Discipleship in the New Testament." *Theology and Life* 9 (1986) 11-24.

Kingsbury, Jack Dean. "On Following Jesus: The 'Eager' Scribe and the 'Reluctant' Disciple (Matthew 8:18-22)." *New Testament Studies: An International Journal of Missionary Research* 12 (1988): 45-59.

LePeau, Andrew T. *Paths of Leadership*. Downers Grove, IL: InterVarsity Press, 1983.

Lincoln, C. Eric. *The Black Church Since Frazier*. New York: Schoken Books, 1974.

_____. *The Black Experience in Religion*. Garden City, NY: Anchor Press/Doubleday, 1976.

_____. *This Road Since Freedom*. Durham, NC: Carolina Wren Press, 1990.

Lincoln, C. Eric, and Lawrence H. Mamiya. *The Black Church in the African Experience*. London: Duke University Press, 1990.

Logan, Sadye M. *Social Work Practice with Black Families*. New York: Longman, 1990.

McLain, Clifford Eugene. *Until the Men Sit Down*. Kansas City: Jordan Communications Company, 1988.

Madhubuti, Haki R. *Black Men: Obsolete, Single, Dangerous?* Chicago: Third World Press, 1990.

_____. *Exploring the Negative Impact of the Black Man's Guide to Understanding the Black Woman*. Chicago: Third World Press, 1990.

Mays, Benjamin E. *The Negro's God*. New York: Atheneum, 1968.

_____. *Quotable Quotes of Benjamin E. Mays*. New York: Vantage Press, 1983.

Milne, Douglas. "Mark: The Gospel of Servant Discipleship." *The Reformed Theological Review* 49 (1990): 20-29.

Moltmann, Jurgen. *Hope for the Church: Moltmann in Dialogue with Practical Theology*. Edited and translated by Theodore Runyon. Nashville: Abingdon Press, 1979.

Moore, T. M. "Education for Christian Discipleship: A Concept and Tool." *Christian Education Journal* 9 (1989): 71-83.

National Urban League, Inc. *The State of Black America 1989*. New York: The National Urban League, 1989.

_____. 1990. *The State of Black America 1990*. New York: The National Urban League.

_____. 1990. *The State of Black Cleveland*. Cleveland: The National Urban League.

Nelson, William R. *Ministry Formation for Effective Leadership*. Nashville: Abingdon Press, 1988.

Nouwen, Henri. *The Way of the Heart: Desert Spirituality and Contemporary Ministry*. New York: Ballantine Books, 1981.

Oden, Thomas C. *Pastoral Theology: Essentials of Ministry*. San Francisco: Harper & Row Publishers, 1983.

Pazdan, Mary M. "Nicodimus and the Samaritan Woman: Contrasting Models of Discipleship." *Biblical Theology Bulletin* 27 (1987): 145-148.

Perry, Bruce. *Malcolm X: Last Speeches*. New York: Pathfinder Press, 1989.

Proctor, Samuel D. *Crisis in the Community*. Philadelphia: The Westminister Press, 1988.

Radamacher, Earl. *The Nature of the Church*. Chicago: Moody Press, 1978.

Rice, Gwendolyn. "Young Black Men, the Church, and Our Future." *Chicago Theological Register* 878 (1988): 10-15.

Roberts, J. Deotis. *Roots of a Black Future: Family and Church*. Philadelphia: The Westminister Press, 1980.

_____. *Black Theology in Dialogue*. Philadelphia: The Westminister Press, 1987.

Rogers, J. A. *One Hundred Amazing Facts About the Negro with Complete Proof*. St. Petersburg, FL: Helga M. Rogers Publishing, 1985.

Roundtree, Leon B. "A Band of Men." *AME Zion Quarterly Review* 102 (1987): 49.

Segovia, Fernando. *Discipleship in the New Testament*. Philadelphia: Fortress Press, 1985.

Sharp, Earle, and Ronald Sunderland. *Biblical Basis for Ministry*. Philadelphia: Fortress Press, 1988.

Shultz, Samuel R. "A Goal-Directed Model for Disciple Making." *Covenant Quarterly* 48 (1989): 28-37.

Skinner, John. *The Christian Disciple*. Latham, MI: University Press of America, 1984.

Smith, Glen G. *Evangelizing Blacks*. Wheaton, IL: Tyndale House Publishers, 1988.

Smith, Wallace C. *The Church in the Life of the Black Family*. Valley Forge, PA: Judson Press, 1985.

Staples, Robert. *Black Masculinity: The Black Male's Role in American Society*. San Francisco: The Black Scholar Press, 1982.

Suso, Henry. *The Life of the Servant.* Translated by James M. Clarke. Cambridge: Clark, 1982.

Tillapaugh, Frank R. *Unleashing the Church.* Ventura, CA: Reval Books, 1982.

Wallace, Darryl. "Jesus Ain't Got No Feet: A Black Perspective on Christology." *Urban Mission* 21 (1989): 13-23.

Washington, James M. *A Testament of Hope: The Essential Writings of Martin Luther King, Jr.* San Francisco: Harper & Row, 1986.

Watson, C. Daniel, J. Christian Baker, and W. Malcolm Clark. *Commitment with Ideology.* Philadelphia: Pilgrim Press, 1973.

Watson, David. *Called and Committed: World-Changing Discipleship.* Wheaton, IL: Harold Shaw Publishers, 1982.

Welsing, Francis Cress. *The Isis Papers: The Keys to the Colors.* Chicago: Third World Press, 1991.

Willard, Dallas. *Spirit of Discipling.* New York: Harper Collins, 1988.

Williams, Preston N. "An African American Perspective on the Unity of the Church and the Renewal of Human Community." *Mid-Stream* 35 (1989): 336-346.

Wilmore, Gayraud S., and James H. Cone. *Black Theology: A Documentary History 1966-1979.* New York: Orbis Books, 1979.

Wilson, Earl D. *The Undivided Self: Bringing Your Whole Life in Line with God's Will.* Downers Grove, IL: InterVarsity Press, 1983.

Wimberly, Edward P. *African American Pastoral Care.* Nashville: Abingdon Press, 1991.

Woodson, Carter G. *The Mis-Education of the Negro.* Washington, DC: Associated Publishers, 1933. Reprint, Nashville: Winston-Derek Publishers Group, Inc., 1990.

About the Author

A native of Ohio, Dr. Larry L. Macon graduated from Cleveland State University in 1973 and went on to receive both his M.A. and his Doctor of Ministry Degrees from Ashland Theological Seminary in Ashland, Ohio. His education and training in African American religious studies have proved invaluable to his work as pastor of the Mt. Zion Baptist Church in Oakwood Village, Ohio. Dr. Macon also serves as Adjunct Professor of Religion at Cleveland State University and president of the United Pastors in Mission, and he is the chairman of the Cleveland chapter of the Southern Christian Leadership Conference. He currently lives in Bedford Heights, Ohio with his wife and their two sons.